ABOUT THE AUTHOR

AARON KARO is the author of *Ruminations on College Life* and *Ruminations on Twentysomething Life*, and has been writing his celebrated email column *Ruminations* since 1997. Also a nationally headlining comedian, Karo has performed on *The Late Late Show with Craig Ferguson* on CBS, and Comedy Central Records released his latest stand-up album, *Just Go Talk to Her,* in 2008. Originally from New York, Karo lives in Los Angeles, where he runs Ruminations.com, the web site he founded to make sure no one gets anything done at work.

I'M HAVING MORE FUN THAN YOU

I'M HAVING MORE FUN THAN YOU

AARON KARO

!t

*it***books**

AN IMPRINT OF HARPERCOLLINS PUBLISHERS

*it**books*

HarperCollins books may be purchased for educational, business, or sales promotional use. For information please write: Special Markets Department, HarperCollins Publishers, 10 East 53rd Street, New York, NY 10022.

FIRST EDITION

Designed by Jaime Putorti

Special thanks to Crown Bar and feedamodel.com

Library of Congress Cataloging-in-Publication Data is available upon request.

ISBN 978-0-06-180521-9

09 10 11 12 13   OV/RRD   10 9 8 7 6 5 4 3 2 1

For all the girls I've ever hooked up with.
I'll never forget you.
That's a lie.

CONTENTS

Earlier this year, as my thirtieth birthday drew closer, I noticed that the women around me wanted to get married more, but I actually wanted to get married *less*. My reluctance to tie the knot is far from an isolated phenomenon; I've observed more than a few guys in their late twenties and early thirties who are enthusiastically unattached — and the women who are increasingly frustrated by them. It strikes me as hilarious, ironic, and a bit cruel that men eschew commitment just when girls begin to crave it most.

You see, I used to think my college years were the best life was ever going to get. Then, I thought I peaked during the frenzied days of my early twenties. But the truth is, I'm just now entering my prime. Turning thirty ushers in a period of unprecedented independence for men. We finally have the confidence, experience, and wherewithal to pursue the lifestyle and the women we desire most. These same women often ask me why the guys they meet are so opposed to the idea of being committed. And I tell them it's because we're just now getting the hang of being single.

As we grow older, it becomes increasingly difficult to avoid comparing ourselves to our peers. After all, I'm bombarded with Facebook alerts whenever my friends (or random acquaintances, for that matter) celebrate a birthday, and I can't help but notice their profile pictures now include a significant other. Invitations to high school reunions beckon and soon I'm being introduced to the husbands and wives of people I never thought would copulate. I flip through the pages of my college alumni magazine and begin to imagine the babies in the photos my classmates submit are smirking at me in disdain. I sit at the singles table at weddings, so far from the action I can barely make out who's delivering the toast I care nothing about. All around me, couples—consciously or otherwise—make those not in relationships feel ostracized, belittled, and unworthy. But all those who cast judgment should take heed of my simple message: "I'm having more fun than you."

Any salute to singlehood is also a celebration of freedom. To me, the advantages of flying solo include not just the ability to pursue any woman, anytime, anywhere (though that's certainly a bonus). The true benefits of bachelorhood are just as much about what you *don't* have as what you do have—one cannot truly live the dream without both the presence of options *and* the absence of annoying obligations to a significant other. Only when those conditions are met can I endeavor to work hard and play harder. I'm not responsible for anyone but myself. And so, simply put, in my life every morning is a morning after.

There are times, however, when I feel a certain kinship with my betrothed brethren. Even though I refuse to be tied down, I can still relate on some level to those who have made the plunge. I guess, in a way, happily married people and perpetually single people are similar: we've both given up on dating and have merely chosen different exit strategies.

These revelations have come after a long and eventful journey. I was born and raised in Plainview, New York, and attended the University of Pennsylvania. It was during my freshman year at Penn that I first began recording the mating and dating rituals of my peers in an email column called *Ruminations*. It went viral, and when I went to work at a major investment bank following graduation, I even listed the far-from-PC column on my résumé. (One day I'll tell my kids how fast and loose those dot.com boom days were.) One year later, in 2002, I found my calling. And it did not involve knowing all the keyboard shortcuts in Excel. That summer I published my first book, *Ruminations on College Life*, performed stand-up for the first time, and left Wall Street forever. Three years later, in the summer of 2005, I was touring the country as a headlining comedian, I published my second book, *Ruminations on Twentysomething Life*, and I defied every fiber of my being by moving from Manhattan to Los Angeles. The allure of touching fake breasts was far too great to resist. Another three years later, in the summer of 2008, I was performing on the *Late Late Show with Craig Ferguson* on CBS, recording an album for Comedy Central Records, and launching Ruminations.com, which enabled my fans to write and share their own twisted thoughts. I review my background here not to impress but rather to impart to you that the book you're about to read is the result of more than a decade's worth of observation and experience. I've spent my entire adult life talking with, partying with, and trying to sleep with my fans across the country. Their stories have inspired me. In fact, I continue to write *Ruminations* to this day. The column, which was first emailed from my dorm room to twenty high school friends, has now been read by hundreds of thousands of people around the world.

This book is about bachelorhood on the brink of thirty. I look back at the hijinks and hook-ups that filled my twenties and look forward to what lies ahead. My lifestyle affords me the opportunity to take risks, make mistakes, and only learn a lesson half the time. And yours can too. But this book won't tell you how to do it, only how I did. What am I, fucking Oprah? Many a night I've found myself reading emails written to me by guys on their BlackBerrys at bars halfway across the country, asking me to give them real-time advice on how to pick up chicks. I usually read those emails on my own BlackBerry while at the bar myself and wondering the exact same thing.

From an objective perspective, one might describe me as a "catch." I'm a successful writer. I have an amazing family that I'm close with and incredible friends who allow me to poke fun at them in print without their consent. I've traveled the world. I possess a sense of humor and an Ivy League degree. I'm also really humble. But all of these things make me one of the most frustrating breeds of men for chicks to deal with: the catch who doesn't want to get caught. The ineligible bachelor. Always the groomsman, never the groom. I want to make clear, though, that this is a conscious decision. I've had serious girlfriends. I've held hands in public. But in the end I always felt constrained, like when you stop short in a car and the seat belt tightens up. More and more often I find myself wanting to just park the car, leap out, and bang a chick whose last name I do not know.

What I find so fascinating about twentysomethings and thirtysomethings is that there seems to be no middle ground — the experience is universally divided. Some of us worry about dying alone. The rest of us fret about going home alone. Some of us fantasize about walking down the aisle. The rest of us revel in doing the walk of shame. Some of us dream about settling down. The rest of us scheme about hooking up. In short, if you're looking for Mr. Right, you've got the wrong guy. I'm Mr. Right Now. Seriously — your place or mine?

The simplest way to gauge where you stand in this conflict is to see who's left when the lights go on after the bar announces last call. If you're still there, you're one of us. If you already left because you found a willing warm body, you're one of us. If you already left because you can't stay up past 1 a.m. and have "brunch" in the morning, you're definitely having less fun than me.

I would also like to state for the record that this book is not an anti-marriage treatise. Do I want to get married some day? Abso-fuckin'-lutely. Just not anytime soon. I'm more than content playing the field. Besides, good things come to those who wait. Like lots of random blow jobs. So don't let it get to you when you see your friends coupling off. Obsessing over that is what makes people our age unhappy. I've seen it firsthand. If you haven't been blessed with the natural disposition to live large, then drink big. No harm has ever come from being single and seeing double. And when your thirtieth birthday comes around, make sure you go out with a bang. Literally.

In addition to freedom, independence, and boundless sexual variety, being single offers another advantage that doesn't get talked about much. Couples deny it and single people themselves rarely realize it. But the fact is, being alone is an incredible opportunity to learn about yourself. You'd be amazed at how not relying on anyone else not only builds character, but also helps you recognize your weaknesses. And only after you are armed with that knowledge do I believe you can truly find the person right for you. At the end of the day, the world between college and marriage isn't easy. During the times that suck, take a step back, look at yourself, and laugh. During the times that are awesome, take lots of pictures because you won't remember shit in the morning. And, finally, to all the single people in the world under thirty, please accept this book as your guide to the road ahead. May your answer to the question "Do you want another drink?" be the only time you have to say, "I do."

CHAPTER 1

SPURNING THIRTY

He who is of calm and happy nature will hardly
feel the pressure of age.
PLATO

When I turned twenty, I was studying abroad in London. It was anticlimactic as far as birthdays go because I was already two years over the local drinking age, and in an era before Facebook, BlackBerry, and Skype, I didn't initially hear from many of my friends back home. I remember feeling very depressed, followed by imbibing many, many pints at the pub, but after that I don't remember very much at all. Looking back ten years later, it's laughable to think I had anything to feel down about. I was still in college, I had my whole life ahead of me, and I was surrounded by chicks with sexy if unintelligible accents. Ironically, my thirtieth birthday was not nearly as traumatic. Whether it was newfound maturity (doubtful) or merely denial (more likely), I began to look at things in a whole new light. Thirty can be an earth-shattering milestone, or it can be just a nice, even number and a convenient age at which to take stock. Either way, an analysis of my life at this moment is straightforward: I'm the odd man out, increasingly marginalized by an influx of couples, and oftentimes looked down on by those who take life way too seriously. But I press forward nonetheless. It's not that I don't care what other people think; it's that I'm too busy checking out the cute brunette who just walked in to be paying attention.

SINGLED OUT

To me, being single is like having diplomatic immunity. I come and go as I please. I answer to no authority. And if accused of lewd behavior, I can just claim ignorance: "Sorry, I'm not from around here and don't understand this concept you call dating." Thankfully, the world is changing for the better. People are getting married later and later—and that means we now have more time to live our lives the way we want to. Birthdays are not so much deadlines as they are markers on the side of the road that you barely notice because you're having such a blast. Hell, thirty is the new twenty.

An experience that is always strange for me is running into a girl I hooked up with two years ago and finding out she's married now. Because it really forces me to compare what she's been doing for the past two years—meeting her husband, having kids, buying a house—with the bullshit I've been doing for the past two years: having a series of quasi-anonymous one-night stands and getting obnoxiously drunk at my friends' weddings. Each time, I consider these facts and contemplate my life and get really introspective. But the conclusion I draw is always the same: thank God I'm not married.

THE SINGLE CALENDAR

Valentine's Day is a holiday—if you can even call it that—when couples are encouraged to rejoice in their relationships while single guys secretly make fun of them. For me, Valentine's Day is like Columbus Day: it has no bearing on my life and I usually only find out about it the day before.

What many women don't realize is that single guys have special powers. I could be in a car with a bunch of married dudes and say, "Holy shit. Did you guys just see that chick? She was fucking gorgeous!" And the married guys are like, "Karo, that car drove by at sixty miles an hour. How did you see anything?" And I say, "I don't know. I guess I just kinda *felt* that she was hot. I must have spider-sense or something. My balls are tingling."

Bachelorhood should be a celebration of independence and, in that vein, I don't think a guy can truly revel in his availability unless he lives alone. Even if you live with just one other single dude, you're still sharing. Sharing is the enemy of the bachelor. Pure, unadulterated selfishness is where it's at. The only downside to living alone in my one-bedroom is that I can't seem to finish a loaf of bread before it spoils, and when I do polish off something, like a big jug of olive oil, I realize it was me alone who ingested the entire thing. Of course, the upside to living alone is being able to do whatever the fuck I want. My refrigerator has a drawer labeled "fresh produce." That's where I keep the beer.

THE SEVENTH WHEEL

In 2007, I had dinner with six friends—two married couples and one couple who lived together—thereby making me the seventh wheel. I'd been the third and fifth wheels plenty of times, but never the seventh. Though I've watched my wingmen being picked off since college, I didn't realize until then how quickly they were all turning to the Dark Side. My high school friends, who've done their share of damage? Half of them are now married. My fraternity brothers, whom I hold up as the modern paradigm of lechery? Nearly two-thirds have been taken out back and shot. Becoming a seventh wheel, it now seems, was inevitable.

Going out that night with my buddies and their wives and girlfriends did give me pause. On one hand, it's kind of depressing to see my friends with their significant others laughing and sharing, and realize I don't have that kind of companionship. On the other hand, it's exhilarating to know that I'm not accountable for anyone's happiness but my own, and that the next girl I wake up beside will quickly realize that's her cue to leave. Upon reflection, I look at being an odd-numbered wheel as a badge of honor. I'd be the fifteenth wheel if I could—if only to be in a room with fourteen people whose lives are less thrilling than mine.

Men and women tend to treat their seventh wheel status differently—the former bask in it while the latter are mortified by the mere prospect of it. I see being surrounded by couples as a positive thing—it's more obvious that I'm available. But for many women, the same situation only makes it more obvious that they're alone. That self-conscious feeling is the result of an unfair stigma foisted upon the fairer sex by society. And by "society" I mean boring married people. Being the odd wheel doesn't have to feel odd. I say if you're young and you're free, enjoy. Rock out and drink up.

There are also times when being a seventh wheel comes with fringe benefits. For instance, when my friends' wives take pity on me because they think I can't fend for myself (which is only partially true). It takes a special kind of guy to let another man's wife cook him dinner and hem his clothing. Besides, who am I to turn down all the perks of marriage while avoiding the cohabitation and monotonous sex?

THE DATING GAME

I've never been much of a dater. I could probably count the number of official dates I've ever been on. Quite frankly, I just don't have the patience. Drinks are for getting drunk, and I prefer to eat dinner while wearing something with an elastic waistband. As far as conversation, well, no one likes to talk about themselves as much as I do, but listening to some chick ramble on about her career as an event planner? No thanks. Besides, it's not a real job if you can be rendered obsolete by an Evite.

The last time I spoke to my buddy Claudio, he was dating four women simultaneously—none of whom knew of the others' existence. Although I admire Claudio's status as a player, his situation doesn't appeal to me at all. I just don't have the patience or the follow-through to keep the game going. Before I tackle dating four girls, I should probably try hooking up with the same girl four times and see how that goes.

What is "dating" anyway? Because I look at it as something you do *after* you've hooked up. It's very rare that I go on a proper first date with a chick that I haven't already banged. Doing things in that order makes the eventual date less awkward and ensures that you have at least some measure of chemistry. Plus, who wants to have dinner with someone you've never seen naked?

STAGE FRIGHT

I once went out with a girl and later gave her some tickets to a stand-up performance of mine. She proceeded to show up with another guy—on another date! The only thing less classy would have been if she started heckling me.

Television's unrealistic portrayal of dating is partly to blame for my aversion to the ritual. No guy in the real world ever says, "So, pick you up at eight?" without giving any indication of what the plans actually are, or how he even knows where the girl lives. Plus, have you ever noticed that when thirty-somethings go on dates on TV, the guy is always wearing a suit and tie and picking the chick up at her brownstone? What universe is this based on? I've never even met anyone who lives in a brownstone. And if I'm wearing a suit, somebody better be getting married or buried (not that there's much difference).

I remember that feeling in the air at my first fraternity date party in college, when all the guys were scrambling at the last minute to figure out whom to ask and what to wear. I still get that feeling every time I go on a date or buy a girl a bottle of wine. Life to me has never ceased to be like one big game of childhood dress-up. Taking a girl to dinner is just about the most mature thing I've ever done. When I'm in the middle of a date I can't help but think I'm still eighteen and soon everyone is going to expose me as a fraud.

The logistics of dating also pose an enormous obstacle for someone as neurotic as myself. If I'm going out to dinner in Los Angeles, my first issue is parking. I can find the restaurant OK, but once I get there I can't park and end up driving in radiating concentric circles until I find a spot a mile away from my initial destination. The girl probably thinks she's in the midst of a kidnapping attempt and I'm trying to disorient her. And parallel parking, forget about it. When I first moved to LA, I was driving an SUV for the first time in my life. I was always scared and unsure about how much space I needed. I swear I parked like a gangly adolescent girl self-conscious about her developing new body.

I cringe when I go to a restaurant for the first time and the waiter asks if I've eaten there before. Because I know that if I answer truthfully, I'll then be subjected to a ten-minute instructional lecture on the intricate aspects of ordering tapas. Listen, if your menu is so complicated that living on earth for thirty years doesn't give me sufficient knowledge to order from it properly, I'm probably not going to like any of this weird-ass food anyway.

When the check comes, there should be absolutely no debate: I'm paying. Ladies, any guy who doesn't pay for you is fucking worthless. Any guy who offers to split the check should hand in his man badge and have his testicles confiscated at the door: he's done. If we make it a few more dates, personally I appreciate when the girl does the fake, reach-for-her-purse move. I'm still paying, but I respect the fact that she's playing along. A few more dates and, yes, I will let the girl pay. But only if she insists. I know I've been spending a shitload of money on her the past few weeks. I also know she's spent a shitload of money on clothes, makeup, waxing, manicures, and other crap I can't even consciously perceive, but all of which collectively made me want to go out with her in the first place.

THE SET-UP

In the twelve years I've been writing my *Ruminations* column, I've received a staggering number of emails—from soldiers overseas thanking me for giving them a laugh to a fan who quoted me while proposing to his girlfriend (apparently he was a hopeless romantic, emphasis on *hopeless*). But I'm always surprised when I receive emails from mothers and fathers trying to set me up with their daughters, and chicks trying to set me up with their girl friends. Apparently, everyone is fair game for being set up these days. It's also interesting how every mother describes her daughter as "gorgeous." Somehow that seems unlikely.

I almost always regret allowing my friends to set me up. Because I've found that friends who know you best are the worst at setting you up. Perfect strangers are much better at it because they don't overthink things. For instance, my tastes are very clear: I prefer brunettes, I like girls in wife-beaters, and I've got a thing for doctors. But that does *not* mean you can only set me up with brown-haired surgeons wearing beaters. If the chick is just hot, she'll do. I'll bang a blonde. Let's not get picky.

A woman will tell you everything about one of her friends, but leave out the most important part: "You have to meet my friend, she's gorgeous, you'll love her." I respond, "Is she single? No? Then who the *fuck* cares?" Ladies, *lead* with that information! What do I want to meet a chick with a boyfriend for? What, are me and her gonna become friends? Read *Us Weekly* and eat nonfat frozen yogurt and share lip gloss and go shopping for candles and ballet flats? Don't introduce me to chicks with boyfriends. You might as well introduce me directly to the boyfriend. The net result is the same: no pussy for me.

> ### OBSERVATION
>
> How long a girl stresses the word "so" when describing how cute her friend is is inversely proportional to how cute her friend actually is. For instance, if a girl is like, "You have to meet my friend Ashley; she's soooooo cute!" that chick is busted.

My guy friends don't get very creative when they're thinking of girls to set me up with. Once my frat buddy Scott asked me, "Karo, you want me to introduce you to this chick Susan? She's pretty hot." "I guess," I said. "How do you know her?" And Scott was like, "I fucked her." That's not really thinking outside the box. But the thing is, that didn't even deter me. I contemplated it for a moment and then asked, "Well, how long ago did you fuck her?"

MATCHMAKER

My single female friends always want me to set them up but it's so annoying. My friend Jen recently asked me to set her up with a buddy of mine she thought was cute. I said, "Sure. I'll just shoot him an email, I'll talk you up, and then I'll have him friend you on Facebook." Jen responded, "Oh, I don't have Facebook." And I said, "Well, I'm not setting you up then." When she asked why, I asked how the hell my guy friend was supposed to stalk her first if she doesn't have Facebook.

Before my buddy would agree to ask her out, he needed to see several pictures of her from multiple angles and at least one photo album from Halloween to see how slutty she dressed. That's the basic starter package.

Then I tried to set up my friend Deb. I was on the phone with her as she was looking at pictures of her prospective suitor when she asked, "Does your friend have blue-green eyes?" I was stunned for a moment then exclaimed, "I don't fucking know what color eyes my friends have! I don't know what color eyes my mom has! I don't know what color eyes *I* have!" When the line went silent, I said, "OK, I mean, do you have a thing for a specific eye color? I guess that's reasonable." Deb responded, "No, but my psychic said that I would meet a guy with blue-green eyes." Seriously? Did your psychic also predict that I would call you a fucking moron?

ZODIAC FILLER

I can't believe there are women out there who still read their horoscopes. "He's a Leo and I'm a Sagittarius. It's perfect!" No guy has ever fucked a chick he met at a bar and then thought to himself, "Well, I guess our moons were aligned."

Most guys know at least one girl that they only keep in touch with because she has a lot of hot friends. There's nothing more disappointing than when I call up my go-to gold mine and her friends can't hang out, but she can. But what frustrates me most is when a girl tells me that her cute friends are single but "not looking." Single but not looking? What the fuck is that? "Well, you know," she says, "if the right guy came along . . ." Every chick's "not looking" until the "right guy" comes along! So basically what you're saying is *I'm* not the right guy. Fair enough.

When one of my guy friends gets set up with a chick who is supposedly very attractive and went to Penn or is from Long Island, and he calls me to ask if I know her, I'm always really chagrined if I don't. If a dude is looking to me for confirmation and I can't provide it, I'm the one who looks bad. Guys are supposed to have radar lock on every hot girl with a given background or within a twenty-mile radius. I'll never admit I don't know her, so I'm just vague and evasive. I'll make shit up like, "Uh, yeah, she sounds familiar. I think my friend banged her once." Then of course he asks me how long ago my friend banged her.

REAL WOMEN THROW CURVES

As someone who is naturally prone to observation, I find the study of women to be a particularly frustrating endeavor. The more I know about them, the less I understand. Nothing defines the difference between men and women more than our relationships with members of the same sex. A woman moved in across the hall from a girl friend of mine and she confessed to me, "I hate my new neighbor; she's so thin and cute." Imagine if a guy moved in next door to me, and I was like, "I totally hate my new neighbor; his hair is so straight and perfect!"

Why do women get upset when you're hooking up and don't notice their "new pretty bra and underwear"? Yes, I know we've been dating for several months, but I still couldn't pick your thongs out of a lingerie lineup. I've been trained since puberty to consider bras and panties mere speed bumps on the road to glory. They are to be smote as quickly as possible without regard to make or model.

OUT OF THE MOUTHS OF BABES

While it's surprised even me that most of the stereotypes about people in Los Angeles aren't true, you would still not believe some of the statements I've heard from chicks in this fair city.

From a girl in my apartment building whom I overheard telling her friend about a new all-liquid diet: "Yeah, it's pretty good, but you kind of miss the chewing."

From a chick I hooked up with, when I asked her if she liked LA: "Well, sometimes I just want to go away for a year to someplace warm." (It was eighty-one degrees in November at the time.)

And, possibly my all-time favorite, from a girl I was walking with in the Hollywood Hills, through a beautiful but heavily wooded area: "Oh my God! This totally reminds me of Rainforest Cafe!"

I once met a girl at a party who clearly had fake breasts. Later, my friend told me that she was a virgin. This annoyed me. Virgins shouldn't have fake breasts. In fact, if you have implants before intercourse, I think you should get an asterisk on your V-card.

I also don't trust a woman with the number 2000 in her email address. If she chose it after the millennium, it demonstrates a lack of creativity. If she chose it before the millennium, well, she really wasn't looking too far ahead. Chicks should also never, ever use text or IM abbreviations in real life. Newsflash: LOL and OMG are not real words. Say them out loud again and I'll TTYL.

WHAT A GUY WANTS

Guys typically have unreasonable expectations. It's not unusual, when asked if a girl is attractive, for a guy to tell his friend, "She's cute, but if she lost, say, thirty-five pounds, she'd be slammin'." In our heads, we actually believe that this is both a reasonable request and an easily attainable goal. On the other hand, guys will steadfastly refuse to change anything—our weight, our hair, or our underwear—to satisfy a chick's slightest preference. Our appearance is nonnegotiable, no matter what the consequences.

We can also be unapologetic dicks. I was in a bar once when I saw a girl I knew back in the day but hadn't seen in a while. I said to a mutual friend, "Hey, is that Leslie? She looks amazing." And my buddy said, "Yeah, she was actually sick for a while. She had really bad mono; like she almost died." I said, "Damn, that's the best thing that ever happened to her!"

ODE TO A WIFE-BEATER

What do I look for in a girl? Is it a sense of humor? A certain body type? Shared interests? No. I'm really just looking for someone in a wife-beater. I think chicks in beaters are incredibly sexy. That's my thing. Now, just to be clear, a wife-beater is white. If you're wearing anything but white, or anything with rhinestones or designs of any kind, that's not a beater, it's a fucking tank top. I'm talking about the kind of beaters you get at Target in a pack of three for $9.99. A beater is not just an article of clothing, it's a statement. A chick in a wife-beater is saying, "I don't care what you think." She's saying, "I don't need fancy clothes to look hot." But most of all she's saying, "Hey you, stranger, look at my tits."

I love how some women actually think they look cuter in glasses. Um, no. The whole time, all I'm doing is imagining what it would be like to fuck you without your glasses. Some girls wear glasses even if they don't need them. What, do I have a librarian fetish? And to the chicks who *do* need a prescription: quit being so goddamn lazy. If I can have lasers burn fucking holes in my eyes, you can throw in some contacts in the morning.

Ultimately, what guys absolutely do *not* want is drama. For instance, I kinda wanna bang the chick who cuts my hair. But I'm forced to balance that notion with the possible fallout. Afterward, would I ever be able to get my hair cut there again? Does she seem like the clingy type? Those scissors *do* look sharp. The last thing I want to do is risk upsetting her and leave our next appointment with a mohawk or, worse, one less ear than I came in with.

IT AIN'T EASY DATING ME

I would be lying if I said that the lack of success I've had with romantic relationships was due solely to the irrational behavior of the women I've dated. I'm acutely self-aware and can admit that getting along with me is no piece of cake. I can be neurotic and downright strange. For instance, I sometimes Google misspelled words to find web sites with poor proof-readers. When using a new bathroom, I often search for the little indent where the doorknob keeps hitting the same spot on the wall. I'm not really a lover or a fighter. I fret, worry, observe, write, and repeat. In essence, when it comes to rela-tionships, it's not that I'm high maintenance, per se; it's more like there's no instruction manual and they stopped making the parts.

Another wonderful trait I have is noticing little things about people—a certain word they use, an idiosyncrasy or flaw they possess—and then calling it to their attention, thus making them incredibly self-conscious. Then I profusely apologize for doing it. Finally, after the issue has long since been forgotten, I get drunk and bring it up again, thus aggra-vating old wounds. After apologizing yet again, I usually make another comment about the person's clothes, career, or hygiene, and the pattern continues.

NEAT FREAK

Some might say I'm a tad obsessive-compulsive. When I was a little kid I went to this museum that had a piece of, like, four-thousand-year-old glass that you could touch. People were amazed at feeling something that our ancestors had created so long ago. But all I remember thinking about is how many other people had touched it since.

My cell phone number happens to be comprised of multiple variations of the numbers six and nine. When I give my number to chicks, they look at me like I'm a dirty bastard. Some guys get a bad reputation from sleeping around. I got mine from T-Mobile.

The people tanning at the pool in my apartment complex in LA always look like they're in such anguish. Is that supposed to be relaxing? Perhaps I'm just jealous because I've recently come to terms with the fact that I am the palest motherfucker in the state of California. The problem is, being in the sun doesn't help because I just go from white to burnt without any browning in between. I seem to carry the recessive gene for tanning but the dominant gene for beer belly.

ACT YOUR AGE

During my five-year college reunion in 2006, I snuck into my old fraternity house, which at the time was being used as some sort of community service dorm. As I wandered about taking pictures, a student approached and asked politely, "Excuse me, who are you?" Instinctively, I turned around and yelled menacingly, "Who the fuck are *you*?" The girl scurried off, but the incident made me wonder if or when I'm ever going to act my age. Consider this: I'm thirty years old, with three books under my belt, regular car insurance payments, and pillowcases that match my comforter. Yet at the same time, I can't drink one beer without drinking twenty, I can't converse with a girl without trying to fuck her, and I can't even step foot in a fraternity house without immediately regressing into an asshole. Am I young at heart or just immature?

The last time I was in Miami, I crashed with my college friends, Jon and Jana, who are now married. We went out and got stupid drunk. I then proceeded to vomit all over their guest bedroom and, when that room proved no longer inhabitable, passed out in the living room on their white leather couch, staining a pillow with the stamp from the bar on my hand. But the worst part was that Jon and Jana didn't really get mad at me. They understood I didn't do it on purpose and I did my best to clean everything up. That really bothered me. The fact that they weren't upset made me feel like their rascally little kid who is always caught up in some hijinks. They *should* be pissed at me. Hell, I'm *older* than they are!

PARTY FOULS

I was at a party once and pulled an Amstel Light out of the fridge. Two of my friends whipped bottle openers out of their pockets. And not sophisticated bottle openers, mind you. I'm talking about the big, round keychain kind with half the paint chipped off and a college logo on it. I was taken aback. Though they're handy, isn't there a cutoff for carrying bottle openers? Junior year, perhaps?

I recently found out that my buddy Jesse has a female roommate. And like most guys, my first question was, "So, do you tap that? Is there some sort of schedule? How does it work?" Of course, they don't hook up. But then I met her for the first time a few days later, and not only is she cute, she's got Civil War cannons. Now, I'm not positive about many things in life. But I am absolutely sure that I'm not mature enough to have a female roommate. Because I would harass the shit out of her. I would come home drunk, bang on her bedroom door, accuse her of leaving her dishes in the sink, offer to let it slide if she blew me, and then wonder aloud what possible downside there could be to roommates with benefits. Then I'd realize she wasn't even in her room and, when confronted by her once she actually did get home, have to admit that I urinated on her door because I thought it was the bathroom. And that would be the first night.

I believe that the real differentiating factor in life—between overgrown adolescents and actual responsible adults—is that adults eat dinner at a real table. They don't sit hunched over their coffee table shoveling heartburn-inducing food into their mouths as fast as possible like most recent college grads and the rest of the animal kingdom. How do the apes at the zoo eat bananas? Hunched over. The amoebas that emerged from primordial ooze? You couldn't tell without a microscope, but they were absorbing nutrients hunched over too. For the first time in my life, my current apartment actually has a dinner table where I can sit and eat. Though it's difficult, I resist the temptation to plop down and eat off the coffee table instead. I interpret this as a sign, albeit subtle, that I'm at least moving in the right direction.

SPURNING THIRTY

One of the scariest parts about turning thirty is looking back to see if you've accomplished anything notable—be it in your personal or professional life—while still in your twenties. I once met a woman a few years older than me at a bar, and we got to talking. She mentioned that before moving to where I live, West Hollywood, she had lived in Malibu for ten years. As she continued, I got distracted because, one, she had enormous fake breasts, and two, I realized that since high school I've never lived in the same state for five years, let alone the same city. In that respect, thirtysomethings today are marked by something our predecessors lacked: transience. We are always on the move, which makes it harder to fall into a rut. In other words, thirty isn't as old as it used to be, so there's no point in wallowing about spending your twenties half-drunk.

Lately, I've noticed a perplexing trend: people assuming that I'm older than I am. When I ask people to guess, they often think I'm in my mid-thirties. I'd like to chalk it up to my precocious demeanor, but I think it's just the fact that I rock perpetual stubble. Further complicating matters is that when I'm occasionally clean-shaven, people think I'm only about twenty-three. So basically I have a complex either way. Happy birthday to me.

FURTHER ENRICHMENT

A woman's age means surprisingly less to guys than most people think. At thirty, I get the same kick out of hooking up with a twenty-five-year-old as I do with a thirty-five-year-old. It's not a woman's actual age that matters to us, it's the *absolute value of the age difference*. A twenty-five-year-old and a thirty-five-year-old hook-up are both five years apart from me and both have distinct but equally appealing attributes—the older chick is more experienced and exotic and the younger chick is more toned and pliable. It's when the absolute value shrinks that I start to get disinterested. No guy wants to bang a girl exactly his own age. What's the fun in that?

I discovered my first gray hair, nestled in my right sideburn, on August 18, 2005, and recorded the date for posterity.

It was a difficult day, but thankfully there haven't been many more sightings since. Not that I haven't been looking. You know you're thirty when you can point out the exact location of each of your gray hairs with your eyes closed.

You also know you're thirty when, for the first time in your life, you turn to your buddy and complain that the bar you're in is "too loud." You know you're thirty when, every once in a while, you turn on *Saturday Night Live* and realize you've never even *heard* of the musical guest. And, painfully, you know you're thirty when *SportsCenter* refers to LeBron James as a "veteran" and you realize he's more than five years younger than you are.

YOUTH MOVEMENT

I know a girl who, when she was twenty-six, was dating a guy still in college. It was weird because I thought most chicks figured out never to sleep at a frat house by the time they were sophomores. What made it even stranger was that, because women mature so much faster than guys do, it's rare to see a young woman dating an even younger man. Guys, of course, are notorious for dating women many years their junior. I'll never forget the time, when I was still living in New York, that my buddy asked me if the bar we were going to that night was checking IDs at the door. Turns out the girl he was seeing at the time was only twenty. I can't chastise him too much, though. Frankly speaking, my wife may still be in high school.

Since I turned thirty, I've had good days and bad, but overall I've remained pretty optimistic. One way to think about it is that, after several years of being in my "late" twenties, I'm now in my "early" thirties. Early is better than late, right? Another way to think about it is to, well, not think about it. Whether you believe thirty is the new twenty, or thirty is the new death, there's nothing you can really do about it. That's why I'm spurning thirty and paying it no mind. People ask me all the time how long I can continue this way of life. Those people are usually sober and annoying. And my response is always the same: "Who the fuck are you?"

THE PATH OF MOST RESISTANCE

Shortly before my thirtieth birthday, I ran into a bunch of guys from my fraternity who were seniors when I was a freshman. I always looked up to these guys—I mean actually looked up to them, as I often lay passed out drunk on the floor of their off-campus apartment. Whenever I would see them after they had graduated, it would be like a glimpse three years into the future for me. When I was a sophomore, they were living in Manhattan and working on Wall Street, as I would later do. By the time I graduated and they were in their mid-twenties, they had started to pursue other interests and disperse across the country, as I would also later do. But now, most of them have moved back to New York, gotten married, and even had kids—none of which I'll be doing in the near future. I'll admit I got a little worried that I might have disrupted the space-time continuum or something. Especially since these guys are all enormously successful and have very hot wives. Then again, their fresh produce drawers are probably stocked with lettuce and shit, which is kinda lame. It dawned on me that diverging from their path may not be the conventional route, but it's definitely the most fun.

MANIFEST DESTINY'S CHILD

The biggest variable in my path has undoubtedly been my move from New York to Los Angeles, where I now live far away from most of the people I've known the longest in my life. One of the oldest running jokes in Los Angeles is that no one is actually born here, they've just moved here from someplace else. I think that's why at parties, when asked how long they've lived in LA, people will often tell you their exact anniversary, like they're recovering alcoholics recounting how long they've been sober: "It'll be twenty-six months next Thursday!"

Among the countless emails from female fans I've received over the years, many have thanked me for providing them with insight into the mind of the twentysomething male. This was never something I set out purposely to do and, quite frankly, if I represented the typical twentysomething male, our entire civilization is fucked. Nevertheless, I wonder if I will be able to duplicate those efforts in my thirties. One could argue that the twentysomething experience is relatively homogenous: move to the nearest big city, work in a cubicle, struggle to pay rent, try to get laid, get a raise, move to another big city, and repeat. At thirty and beyond, however, those parallel trajectories begin to be altered irrevocably. No two paths are the same, which makes it more difficult to generalize. I'm not too worried, though, because when it comes to the opposite sex, some things never change. As you get older, you may stand straighter and walk taller, but the ultimate goal is always to end up horizontal.

CHAPTER 2

AHEAD OF THE GAME

All the world's a stage,
And all the men and women merely players.
WILLIAM SHAKESPEARE

Being in a serious relationship presents a frustrating paradox: you no longer have to work for sex, but you can also only have it with one person. On the other hand, being single means having to pound the pavement just to get some action, though the possible sources of that action are seemingly endless (depending on your standards and the acuity of your beer goggles). We bachelors have chosen to take our chances with the latter scenario. Luckily, we have also developed an arsenal of resources and strategies to help weaken the resolve of the women we encounter. Consequently, women have become adept at thwarting our advances. It's essentially an arms race, with two adversaries stockpiling weapons despite calls from both sides to literally make love, not war. The entire courtship process—hitting on, being hit on, buying drinks, playing coy, lying, texting, thrusting, and parrying—is known collectively as "game." And while I believe it's possible that single men and women actually have an equal desire to hook up, it is the guys who most often act on these instincts, which usually casts us in the role of the aggressor. Our ploys are sophisticated, our angles many, and so the only way for a girl to keep her sanity—and her clothes on—is to stay ahead of the game.

THE APPROACH

Any guy will tell you that the hardest thing of all to do is pick up a completely random chick. Not a friend of a friend, not a girl you kind of know from camp. Just a complete stranger. Because we have absolutely nothing to go on. Which is why I've always wished that chicks had Citysearch reviews. I could spot a girl at a bar and then look her up on my Black-Berry to get the lowdown before approaching her. A review might read: "Michelle is ultra-hip and stylish. Attracts investment bankers with expense accounts. A tight squeeze but open late and accommodating to most requests." I'd contemplate this and then say to my buddies, "I don't know. I'm really looking for something a bit easier to get in to."

Of course, if I were actually able to ascertain any shred of intelligence about a girl in a bar before approaching her, it would be whether or not she's single. The problem is, single guys broadcast their availability while women tend to conceal it. Ask me if I'm single and I'll immediately say yes and then interrogate you about why you're asking and who wants to know. Ask a girl if she's single and she'll invariably stammer, glance at her girl friends, giggle, mention something about some guy in Chicago she's "sorta seeing," and then finally confess she's unattached.

If you're a girl in a bar who has a boyfriend, the law should require that, instead of "hello," the first word out of your mouth be "boyfriend." That would solve so many problems. Me: "Come here often?" You: "Boyfriend." Me: "Let's pretend this never happened." The reason it needs to be the very *first* word she says is that, for some reason, whenever I've spent more than two minutes talking to a girl and then all of a sudden she mentions her significant other, my initial reaction is to start making fun of her boyfriend's name, like somehow that will break them up on the spot. "Ben? You're dating a guy named *Ben*? What kind of name is Ben? Sounds like a really cool guy. Ben? You've gotta be fucking kidding me."

TERMINOLOGY

Throughout this book, I will use the term "game" to refer generally to the art of hitting on a member of the opposite sex. In many parts of the country, kicking game to a chick is also called "macking." However, upon moving to Los Angeles I learned that here the verb "to mack" actually means to physically hook up with someone, not merely flirt with them. So for a while, my boys in LA were under the impression that I was getting laid *all* the time, until they realized I was misusing the term. To avoid further confusion, I will refrain from using "mack" in any context, and hopefully stop my friends from making fun of me.

As I prepare for my approach, I pay careful attention to a woman's hands. Because there I may find one of two red flags that will cause me to abort the mission: an engagement ring or a cigarette. Looking for a ring is a habit that only first became necessary in the latter half of my twenties. Perhaps it's unconscious denial on my part, but most of the time I still forget to do it. And every time I kick myself, because married chicks won't stop you for a while when you hit on them. I think it makes them feel like part of the action. Like they're watching a game show and playing along for fun.

Spying a girl fingering a cigarette runs a close second to spotting a wedding ring in terms of turning me off completely. Smokers are just making it that much harder for themselves, as a chick with a cigarette has to be twice as hot for me to even consider approaching her. I've even been told that I get an involuntary scowl on my face when people smoke nearby. My friend Holly once said, "Karo, I feel worse lighting up in front of you than I would in front of my mom." Apparently I'm giving off the right vibe.

THE NUMBERS GAME

I'm a confident guy but still get nervous around really attractive women, especially when I'm sober. Recently I was in this lounge that I frequent a few blocks from my apartment when a ridiculous chick touched me on the arm and asked if I knew the name of the bar. I stared at her slack-jawed before finally muttering, "I have no idea." Very slick. My buddy Jeff has a term for these girls who are way out of anyone's league. He calls them "uncomfortably hot." This is the rare girl who is so gorgeous, you actually feel awkward around her.

The issue that has plagued men for millennia is how to properly gauge a woman's attractiveness and, more importantly, convey that measurement to his drinking buddies in an efficient manner. Merely describing a girl as "hot" is insufficient. I mean, there's a big difference between the hottest girl who went to my high school and the hottest girl from the last season of *Entourage*. Thus, rating systems were born: mechanisms passed down for generations that enable guys to assign a universally understood numerical value to a girl they see in a bar. The entire exercise is, of course, superficial and borderline offensive. Which is why I'd like to break down the four major schools of thought.

RATING SYSTEMS

SYSTEM	SCALE	BENEFITS	DRAWBACKS
One-to-Ten (a.k.a. "The Classic")	Ten is hot, one is not; the higher the better.	Most popular.	Open to large degrees of interpretation.
Area Code	Three digits: each one to nine. First rates the girl's face, second her body, and third overall.	Most detailed.	Most complicated; borders on doing math.

RATING SYSTEMS (continued)

SYSTEM	SCALE	BENEFITS	DRAWBACKS
Binary	Two choices: zero or one. One means "go for it," zero means "don't."	Simplest.	Only works if both parties have seen the girl in question. (You can't call your buddy the next day and brag about banging a one.)
Beer-Intake Scale	How many beers it would take me to hook up with her; the lower the better.	Combines alcohol with ogling.	Drinking said amount of beers may render the possibility of hooking up moot.

It is considered uncouth for a guy to reveal to a woman her rating. But if a girl somehow comes across this delicate information, it's important that she know which system is being used to rate her. For instance, if she overhears a guy telling his friends that she's a three, she might get really upset. But that's only bad if he's rating her from one to ten. Instead, he may be using the Beer-Intake Scale. Under that methodology, three is pretty good. Unless the dude is a real lightweight, in which case she doesn't want to be messing with him anyway.

Unfortunately, the various systems are not really compatible. It's sort of like Celsius and Fahrenheit. You can convert Area Code to Binary, but it's a complicated formula and, quite frankly, who has the time? There are, however, many subtle-ties and nuances to a girl's rating. For instance, an accent always adds at least one point (notwithstanding those from New York's outer boroughs). I was out to dinner with the boys once and our waitress was British. We spent most of the meal giggling like schoolgirls whenever she spoke and then we left about a 45 percent tip. Shortly thereafter, I was at a wedding and met a girl with a really thick Southern accent. I couldn't tell you what she looks like, but I do know that I love her.

Another variable is geography. Some regions of the country just have better-looking women. A nine in LA is much better than a nine in Minneapolis. A "true Miami eight" is essentially a 9.5 in Boston. This is the same reason why attractive women in smaller or cold weather cities get more attention—there's less competition. Moral of the story: if you're hot in Omaha, don't move.

TENS

When bachelors on the prowl set their sights high, they're looking for the Holy Grail of women—a perfect ten. At first I thought this was just a myth. A girl with a perfect body and perfect face couldn't really exist this side of Megan Fox, could she? I'd performed stand-up in nearly every major American city, but still had not found this elusive bounty. And then I moved to Los Angeles. Bingo.

I've been to fairly low-key bars in LA and still had trouble keeping track of how many "tens" were in the room. It's absurd. I'm not saying I hook up with them, or even talk to them. In fact, I'm saying I don't and I can't. But I'm strangely comforted by the fact that someone must be. Recently I was at a party in Hollywood—hammered—and found myself talking to this ten I had no shot with. I stumbled to the bathroom and, when I returned, resumed the conversation. After a few minutes, I realized that this was actually a different girl. LA has got to be the only place on earth where you can be talking to a ten, and then turn around and start talking to another fucking ten! (And have them both hate you equally.)

FURTHER ENRICHMENT

The International Bureau of Weights and Measures is a real organization, based in Paris, that maintains the official one-kilogram brick and one-meter stick. These are the standards upon which all measurements in the world are based.

Allegedly, in that same little room, next to the brick and the stick, sits a ridiculously hot woman. She's the official perfect ten—the international benchmark for hotness. Her name is Sandra. And you have no shot.

Women of New York, my cherished home state, will always be my first love. But after careful empirical analysis, I have to say the chicks in LA are, on average, much hotter. I'm sorry, but it's true. On the other hand, women in New York (and for that matter, almost everywhere) are more approachable than women in LA. In fact, my frat buddy Ryan even makes the laughable but logical case that the girls in LA are actually *too* hot. Which prompts me to pose an important philosophical question: If a perfect ten walks in the door but no one can talk to her . . . does she exist?

Rating women and scoping out tens are an integral part of the game for guys. Plus, anything with rankings or stats kinda reminds us of sports, so that's a bonus. In the end, though, hitting on chicks is like the NCAA tournament: on any given night there's a chance you could take down someone ranked much higher than you. And that, in a nutshell, is the beauty of being single: you never know what girls the next bar will bring. Hope springs eternal. Still, in the numbers game, the odds are often stacked against you. In college basketball, overcoming those odds is called being Cinderella. Every year, when March Madness unfolds, you hear a lot of gushing over Cinderella. But I'd only rate her about a seven.

THE NAME GAME

I have never met anyone who says they are great with names. Even I catch myself at parties complaining, "I'm just terrible with names." And I'm always met with obedient head nods and murmurs of agreement. The fact is, guys remember the names of women they *want* to remember. If I didn't get your name the first time, and I don't bother asking again, that means I don't give a shit. If I didn't get your name the first time, and I ask you over and over again, that means I'm interested but too wasted to be of any use to you. If I strike up a conversation with you, and blatantly overuse your name ("Wow, that's really great, Jamie. Jamie, what is it you do again, Jamie? Really, Jamie, you're an attorney? I've always been interested in the minutiae of corporate law, Jamie."), that is a telltale sign I'm really into you. Or I have retrograde amnesia.

One of the rarest and most serendipitous things that can occur when I'm kicking game at a bar is meeting two cute girls who are friends and happen to have the same name. I call this "Double Jeopardy." Now I only have to remember one of them. Sometimes I get cocky and give the girls cute nicknames for the night like Lindsey One and Lindsey Two. Of course, then I forget which is which. On the other end of the difficulty scale is meeting a chick with a difficult-to-pronounce name. Ladies, when you introduce yourself, if the guy says, "What?" twice or more, you fall into this category. Now I'm drunk and trying to remember both your name and which vowel the fucking umlaut goes over. This is quickly becoming too much work.

HCIs

For years, I've wondered how it's possible that annoying people who don't shut the fuck up don't realize how annoying they are. We've all been there—trapped in a conversation with someone who isn't able to pick up on the most obvious hints that you're not interested whatsoever in what they have to say and are desperate to leave. I call these people HCIs—"head cock inducers"—because while you're standing there listening to them blab on and on, you subconsciously cock your head to the side and think to yourself, "Is this person fucking serious right now?"

An HCI can be a guy or a girl. Either way, they're always blissfully unaware. It seems like whenever I'm talking to a bunch of women, the least attractive and most annoying one latches on to me. It's kind of like when you go to Hooters and get the one ugly waitress. You sit down, all excited—"Hooters, yeah!"—and then you see the waitress start to walk in your direction and you're like, "Oh no, not her. No [look around], oh no, we wanted Brandi . . . ohhhhh . . . I guess I'll have the buffalo wings."

GLOSSARY

WASTED HAPPY HOUR CHICK

A species of HCI that goes straight from work to happy hour and is still there at midnight even though her colleagues are all gone. Wasted happy hour chicks seem like they should be easy prey, considering they're often found dancing wildly by themselves in the corner. But I'm no longer fooled—there's a reason she's been left unpicked-up. And it's usually the guy in Chicago that she's sorta seeing.

As much energy as I expend chasing appealing women, I spend an equal amount of time avoiding HCIs. Most guys are quite adept at evading girls—which is not surprising given how so many of us seem naturally selected for the very purpose of repelling them. When a girl whom I've been trying to avoid calls me and I accidentally pick up, you would not believe the shit I come up with: "Oh, uh, hey Jill. Where am I? You know what's funny? No one here knows the name of this bar. And there's no sign. And none of the adjacent streets have signs either. But you should—" and then I hang up mid-sentence (which gives it a feel of authenticity), shut off my phone, and pretend the battery died.

Women, of course, have a much more elegant method of avoiding male HCIs—they don't bother talking to them in the first place, a devious tactic I call "preemptive avoidance." When accosted, though, girls are skilled at shutting down unwanted advances. I've found that the less a girl wants to hook up with a guy she meets at a bar, the more outlandish an excuse she'll give, and it will often be accompanied by blatant giggling and eye rolling from her nearby friends. And nothing inspires confidence in a guy like a giggling, eye-rolling girl telling you she has to leave because she's got a placekicking tryout with the Giants in the morning.

THE MINDSET

The truest and most frustrating observation ever made about kicking game is that it's all about confidence. Every guy has contemplated how much damage he could do if he could just go back ten years knowing what he knows now.

But we're stuck with what we've got. Luckily, the desire to hook up outweighs every other one of our primal instincts.

My favorite television show is *Lost*. I'm obsessed with it. There's just something about these flawed characters trapped on a mystical island that totally fascinates me. But there is one important, real-world lesson that I've learned from *Lost*. After all the survivors have been through—the crash, the smoke monster, the Others—they've never, ever given up hope on pulling ass. It's like the first week they were concerned with getting rescued. The second week they were concerned with getting water. And by the third week they were concerned with getting head. Somehow, it always comes back to that.

These pressures aren't unique to us humans. I was recently reading about these insects called cicadas that lie dormant underground for seventeen years. After seventeen years, they come out, they mate, and then they die the next day. And I couldn't help but wonder, how much would it suck to be the guy who doesn't hook up that night?

GLOSSARY

DUCK HUNT
Named for the classic Nintendo game, a Duck Hunt is a bar or situation where girls are shooting guys down right away.

Perhaps the most trying situation I've encountered is going out on the prowl with friends who are in relationships.

I think that the longer you're in a relationship, the more you begin to forget what it was like to have ever been single, and how the game actually works. Whenever I'm in a bar with a couple who I'm friends with, they'll inevitably say, "Hey Karo, check out that girl over there. She's totally cute—you should just go talk to her." Oh, is that all I have to do? Just go *talk* to her? Well, thanks for clearing that up, because I was just gonna whip my dick out and hope she came over and touched it. But just go talk to her? That's a foolproof plan! Is that how you two met? Who knew it was that easy? Thank God I have you and your girlfriend here to show me how the world works. Now stop holding hands and drinking chardonnay, and get the fuck out of my face so I can continue stalking this chick from a distance!

THE COMPETITION

A cute girl once asked me what I thought about a guy across the bar. I told her I thought he was a douchebag. She asked why. I said because any guy besides me whom a girl is interested in is a douchebag. You see, guys generally don't like other guys who are not our friends. But we definitely don't like other single guys who are our competition. It is a well-known fact that women dress to the nines often just to look good in front of other women. Guys compare themselves to other guys as well. Except Brad Pitt could walk in the door and we'd still mutter under our breath, "Douche."

There are many varieties of douchebag, none of whom recognize their fatal flaws. Listen, guys, wearing only a V-neck undershirt to a bar is just not acceptable. Neither is sporting a blazer over said undershirt, unless you're going for the "just went to the dry cleaners but only half my order was ready" look. Also, if you're about to go out but can't remember if you put cologne on, don't give yourself a precautionary spritz. Too much is worse than none. Your cologne should not linger in the elevator any longer than you do. Oh, and if you're actually using water from the sink in the bar bathroom to restyle your hair, you should have never even bothered going out in the first place.

GLOSSARY

THE BAD BASKETBALL GAME THEORY

My old roommate Brian conceived the argument that bad basketball games are a great place to pick up chicks. His thinking is that when two bad teams are playing, dads who have season tickets give their seats away, not to their sons, who presumably know the game will suck, but rather to their hot daughters. Ipso facto, bad basketball games are often filled with hot chicks.

One arena where I'm admittedly deficient when compared to other guys is performing in "nontraditional" situations. Friday and Saturday night is business time, and I dress the part. But even though I'm aware that there are plenty of opportunities to meet women during the week, like on the subway or in the grocery store, my civilian attire is totally lacking. I hate guys who wear nice clothes on Sunday afternoon even if they're not going anywhere. When I look around, dudes are wearing dress shoes, khakis, and polo shirts. Why? It's Sunday. Afternoon. I'm not even wearing socks, let alone something with a collar. But the fact is, they are prepared for chance encounters. Generally speaking, I know I'm not suited to kick game to a beautiful woman when I walk into my apartment building and the doorman mistakes me for a deliveryman.

Shortly after I moved to LA, I had a meeting at MTV's offices in Santa Monica. In the lobby with me were thirty of the hottest fucking chicks I've ever seen, all waiting for an audition. Tens as far as the eye could see—and no male competition in sight. After I stopped my hands from shaking, I called my buddies in New York to apprise them of the situation. They urged me to hit on everything that moved, but before I could gather up the nerve, I got called into my meeting. By the time I got out, the girls were gone. In a way, I'm glad—it would've been a Duck Hunt anyway.

GAME ON

When we're taking the elevator down to the lobby after getting ready to go out for the night, I'm always amazed at how chivalrous my friends and I are. We're holding the door for girls, we're making sure they all get out first, we're generally being polite and friendly. Then we get to the bar and immediately lose all sense of tact and discretion as we vainly make passes at any chick above a six. I really believe that guys would be much better off if we never left the elevator. That option notwithstanding, after I've assessed my options, scouted the competition, and made my approach, the game is officially on.

First things first: there is no such thing as a pick-up line. The kind of guys who use pick-up lines that actually work are the kind of guys who don't need them in the first place (i.e., they've won an Oscar or are Derek Jeter). I've only used two successful lines in my entire life: "I'm in this fraternity; wanna go upstairs?" and "I'm the guy you just saw onstage; wanna go upstairs?" I mean, let's face it, if I ever move to a first-floor apartment, I'm fucked.

Guys should, however, be encouraged to leverage (and embellish) their particular situation for the purposes of game. The most effective scenario is if you've just moved to a new city. "I just moved here" is a trusty icebreaker and conversation-prolonger. It also invites an element of pity that cannot be underestimated. If the new-in-town theme seems to be working, guys will often try the "Let's go back to my place—you can be the first person to see my apartment!" tack. Women should be wary, though, that there is no set statute of limitations. You are most likely *not* the first girl to have seen this dude's apartment. Hell, I moved to Los Angeles years ago and I still break that puppy out every once in a while.

LITERARY ANALYSIS

New York Times bestseller *The Game* by Neil Strauss popularized the concept of "negging." A neg is a comment made to a woman that does not directly insult her, but instead subtly prods her, ostensibly piquing her interest in turn. While negging is indeed an integral part of flirting that most guys utilized prior to *The Game*, it is still a difficult art to master. Here are two examples from my own experience.

CORRECT: LEAVES WOMAN OFF-BALANCE AND SELF-CONSCIOUS

> **CUTE CHICK I RAN INTO ON THE STREET:** Hey Karo!
>
> **ME:** Did you just come from the gym?
>
> **CUTE CHICK:** What? No.

INCORRECT: LEAVES WOMAN INSULTED AND SEARCHING FOR MACE

> **ME:** I'm looking for a shirt for my sister but I have no idea what size.
>
> **CUTE SALESGIRL:** Well, what does she look like?
>
> **ME:** A lot skinnier than you.

One thing that most guys have been blessed with is the ability to sound interested. No matter how dull her job, inane her jokes, or boring her banter, if I'm attempting to get into a girl's pants, I can feign curiosity about whatever the fuck she's talking about. Guys do this because we've found that walking away glassy-eyed in mid-conversation ensures we won't get laid. If you're a girl who majored in communications or likes to show off her iPhone, please be aware that every male you've ever spoken to in your entire life was faking it. Just a heads up.

There is a stark difference, however, between embellishing how long ago you moved or faking like you're paying attention to a girl, and flat-out lying to her. This is an issue that bachelors are evenly divided on. Some get off on it. The bolder the lie, the greater the challenge. Some guys lie because their real life sucks. Others, like me, reject lying as uncool, unfair, and unnecessary. Also, I'm not a very good liar. Besides, it's too easy to go too far. I'll never forget when my buddy Shermdog excitedly told me he'd just met two hot European blondes at the bar and told them we were from Quebec. I said, "Good work, Sherm. But next time you lie and say we're Canadian, I'd avoid the one French-speaking province."

PLAN OF ATTACK

Once a guy has acquired a target and sees potential, he is then faced with maintaining a difficult balance: trying not to smother the girl or appear too interested, while at the same time not losing her either. One of the worst feelings is turning around and realizing the amazing girl I've just met, whose name I can actually remember, is now missing in action. Because drunk chicks are like pinballs: they'll bounce around the bar like ding!—ding!—ding ding!—ding!—ding! and then just go home with the last guy they bump into. So I always try to keep a safe distance while never letting the girl out of my sight. If I lose her, I'm then forced to do a full sweep of the bar because the time and energy consumed establishing rapport with a new girl will be far greater than that required to locate my original mark. Guys must also always be vigilant of "kissing whores"—women who will make out with you on the dance floor and then run over to their friends, giggle, order lemon drops, and hide. You will never see her again, unless you resort to just waiting outside the women's bathroom all night on the off chance that she comes out of hiding or drunkenly knocks into you.

GAME AROUND THE WORLD

One of my favorite places to visit is Japan. Mainly because 90 percent of the chicks in Tokyo are thin, have perfect skin, dress well, and are hot. The downside? They usually don't speak a lick of English. The biggest stumbling block to hooking up in Japan, however, is that they don't have one-night stands there. And when I say they don't have one-night stands, I mean it's just not part of their culture; they don't even understand what a one-night stand is. Whenever I found an attractive girl who spoke passable English, I would of course move in for the kill. The conversation usually went something like this.

> **ME:** Let's get out of here.
> **GORGEOUS JAPANESE CHICK:** What do you mean?
> **ME:** We can head back to my hotel.

> **GJC:** Why? I have my own apartment.
>
> **ME:** So you wanna go back to your place?
>
> **GJC:** Why would you come with me?
>
> **ME:** Um, so we can like, you know . . .
>
> **GJC (FINALLY UNDERSTANDING):** Oh . . . But then I'll never see you again.
>
> **ME (IMPROVISING):** Uh, that's not true. I just moved here for work.
>
> **GJC:** Where do you work?
>
> **ME:** Where do I work? Um, Sanyo.
>
> **GJC:** Did you just read that off the billboard behind me?

Identifying one woman and then focusing all my efforts on her is obviously not the most successful strategy. That's why I've always been impressed with my high school buddy Matt, who's consistently been able to hook up with girls who are—to be honest—much higher rated than he is. I think this is due to several factors: he's a smart, funny dude, he has no shame, and upon getting to the bar he goes right for the girls without wasting any time hanging out with his buddies. At the end of the day, though, Matt's secret weapon is that he plays a different kind of numbers game: hitting on as many chicks as humanly possible during the night, in the hope that the law of averages will produce at least one score. Essentially, he engages in a kind of modified speed dating, except he's the only guy and "dating" is the least of his objectives. I admire his moxie. But I could never duplicate his success. It requires too much effort, too much rejection, and the ability to juggle multiple pseudonyms and fake careers.

Personally, I've found that being completely candid works best in the hook-up game. I'll tell a girl, "Listen, I'm not really from Quebec. In fact, I couldn't even point it out on a map." Women seem to appreciate honesty (short of admitting that I've been utilizing a series of exceedingly complicated rating systems to codify their hotness). They don't appreciate rudeness or pick-up lines. But despite knowing all this, I'm sure the next time I spot an LA eight I'll regress to the tried-and-true "Wanna go upstairs?" And if she responds, "We're already upstairs," I'll know it's time to stop drinking.

THE TEXT BEST THING

There is no doubt that the proliferation of text messaging has made the world a better place. And by "the world" I mean "my world." And by "better" I mean "enhanced my ability to hit on chicks without the risk of face-to-face rejection." In fact, I believe text messaging has already made the booty call completely obsolete, joining the ranks of buying flowers, going out to dinner, writing letters, and engaging in actual conversation as artifacts in the annals of hook-up history.

The first arena in which text messaging aids a bachelor on the prowl is the process of "laying groundwork." One of the things I've learned is that most women don't actually mind one-night stands; *they just don't want it to feel like one.* Laying groundwork simply means initiating contact with a girl via text message approximately one week before contact is likely to take place (for instance, an upcoming party you're both invited to). This weakens the girl's defenses by extending flirtation over a longer time period and making it seem like I'm not just hitting on her out of the blue when we see each other. Groundwork is, in essence, the opposite of a booty call. While a booty call is spontaneous—a shot in the dark fueled by alcohol—groundwork is premeditated and therefore twice as devious and effective.

The death of booty calls has also signaled the birth of booty texting—which is really a completely different animal. Instead of calling girls individually, and most of the time accomplishing nothing more than leaving a slurred voicemail at 2 a.m., now I merely send ten girls a mass text message that just says: "Hey." Most women are aware that if they receive a text message from a guy at 2 a.m. that just says, "Hey," they can safely interpret that to mean, "Wanna fuck?" Of the ten texts I send out, let's say I get four responses back, two are promising, and one girl I take home. There's no way I could achieve that kind of return by actually talking to or calling girls individually. We are truly living in a golden age.

GLITCH IN THE MATRIX

I will never give up my full keyboard BlackBerry. The worst part about my old phone? Texting someone and the predictive feature not being able to recognize the word "texting."

The tricks don't end there. If I'm texting with a girl, and I somehow cross the line, I can always get out of it. If I write, "u wanna come over?" and she replies, "no way asshole," all I have to do is write back: "so sorry, my buddy stole my phone. he was messing around, i didn't write that." I'm telling you, I do it all the time. Texting with a girl is like those old Choose Your Own Adventure books—if you don't like where the story is going, you can always back up and opt for a different path.

If you really want to get sophisticated, here's a method I use to disguise my booty texting. I'll write a message that doesn't really make any sense (such as: "can u pick up some eggs and milk?") and then send it to the girl I'm targeting. She'll read it and respond: "did u mean to send this to me?" And then I'll write back: "oh no, wrong person! so...what are u up to tonight?" *Bam!* I'm in and she doesn't even know what the fuck just happened!

Another text technique I utilize is called "plausible deniability." Basically, if I get really drunk and start texting every girl in my phone, but I don't expect anything to pan out, I'll delete my own outgoing text log just before blacking out for the night. That way, the next day when a girl is like, "Karo, did you fucking text me at six in the morning?" I can say, "Honestly, I have no idea."

FURTHER ENRICHMENT

The ellipsis is an invaluable tool for kicking game via text message. Those three simple dots can say so much. "i thought you wanted to hang out" comes off cold and angry. But "i thought you wanted to hang out..." implies there's room for you to make it up to me (with head).

My latest weapon is two dots. Chicks don't know what the hell to make of it. A girl will text me and I'll write back: "that's what you think.." It's not quite a period, not quite an ellipsis, but it sure as hell keeps 'em on their toes.

As with any powerful tool, text messaging has its short-falls. For instance, there's the dreaded scenario when a girl texts me: "i'm with my bf" and I have no idea if she means "best friend" or "boyfriend." And when a random text pops up on my phone from a number I don't recognize, I immediately Google the area code to determine where in the country the texter resides. This knowledge allows me to not simply delete the message, but instead delete the message while exclaiming, "Who the fuck is texting me from [insert city]?"

In my last book, *Ruminations on Twentysomething Life*, I wrote that if a guy leaves a voicemail for a chick, and she emails him back, that's a pretty bad sign. But if a guy leaves a voicemail for a chick and she *texts* him back, that's even worse. Because that means she had her phone in her hand, and instead of hitting one button to call you back, she hit fifty buttons to text you instead. That's how much she didn't want to talk to you.

Texting is a valuable part of the single guy's arsenal, but sometimes we forget to text in moderation. Recently I found myself lying in bed on a Saturday, nursing a hangover, and texting with a girl to try to get her to come out that night. When the conversation was over, I looked at the clock, saw it was 11:49 a.m., and realized I had set a new personal record: hitting on a chick before noon.

E-GAME

Technology has enabled today's bachelor to minimize the number of physical touchpoints involved between meeting a girl and getting her in the sack. We may be introduced on Facebook and then transfer the conversation to email, before finally making plans via text. Or we may discover each other on Twitter and begin emailing, before meeting up via BlackBerry Messenger. Whatever the scenario, electronic game (or "e-game") is rapidly becoming the most important skill single dudes can possess.

The granddaddy of modern technology—email—is still the cornerstone of all e-game. The first email method I use is called the "solo BCC." Essentially, I write what *looks* like a mass email (for instance, a query if anyone is looking for a roommate), but then only BCC one person—the girl I'm targeting. If I craft the message properly, I can get her to respond—thereby initiating the conversation—without seeming like I was purposely hitting on her.

Once email rapport has begun, I'm careful never to send two messages in a row without her replying first—that reeks of desperation. If the dialogue doesn't seem to be going anywhere, or if it's getting late, I always make sure she sends the final email. That way she's left wondering what happened until I pick up the exchange the following day. She might even send two emails in a row, thus giving me even more of an upper hand.

ETIQUETTE

If you're going to attempt to kick e-game, make sure you have your email set up to include the previous message in your reply. Quite possibly my biggest pet peeve is when girls write me a clean email without the entire thread below. Listen, lady, I'm hitting on several chicks at once here; refreshing my memory about what the hell we were talking about is common courtesy.

In addition, sending me a drunk email is always welcome. But please do not accidentally hit caps lock and then write me a rambling missive in which all the letters that are supposed to be lowercase are capitalized, and vice versa. It looks like a little electronic ransom note.

One of the pitfalls of emailing (and texting) is that it is difficult to discern nuance in the other person's messages. Sometimes I'll be emailing with a girl and the conversation is flirtatious yet also a little adversarial, and so I start to think that there's a lot of sexual tension between the two of us and that, quite possibly, the next time we see each other, all that tension is going to bubble over and we're just gonna fuck like animals. But it usually turns out that it was all in my head and she was being kind of snippy not to be flirty, but because she actually genuinely dislikes me.

Email has also gotten me into trouble. Like many guys, I have a lot of nicknames for women in my cell phone—either girls whose names I don't know, or those whom I felt I would remember better if they were given a descriptive moniker. Some of the nicknames are benign. Others are, you might say, unflattering (e.g., Sergeant Sloppy Tits). Then, several years ago, I got my first BlackBerry. I began emailing away, but soon realized that the girls I was hitting on were either not responding or getting really pissed off. And that's when I realized that when I set up the BlackBerry, it had automatically integrated my cell phone address book with my email address book. So I had been emailing all these girls and their *nicknames were showing up*. Fuck me.

GLOSSARY

WIDECLOPS

Nickname I coined for a girl whose eyes are too far apart. A telltale sign you've spotted a wideclops is that she's looking right at you but you can only see one of her eyes at a time. This specimen is ornery in nature and generally not pleased when you enter her name in your address book as simply "Wideclops" and then accidentally email it to her.

Some girls use instant messaging as their preferred mode of online communication. I rarely use IM because I can't stand to sit there waiting for a response, and most people type (or think) too slow. Plus, I've always hated those cliché sitcom moments when a character is about to drop a bombshell, but just before he does, the other character drops a bigger bombshell of her own and then says, "So, what were you going to say?" Cue awkward, contrived pause and canned laughter. That very situation happens almost every day on instant messenger. Sometimes I'll type a message and am about to hit Send when the other person writes something crazy that makes my unsent response obsolete. I then carefully delete what I was about to send and slowly back away from the computer.

While it's not my favorite technology, I am adept enough at instant messaging that others have outsourced their needs to me. Shermdog, who is most comfortable chatting up women in person, once got an IM from a chick he barely knew. Seeing the conversation going nowhere fast, he asked me to stand behind him and tell him what to type. A few hours later, he was nailing her. Seriously, I'm like an electronic Cyrano.

FRIEND REQUESTS WITH BENEFITS

I'm not one to exaggerate, but Facebook is the greatest thing to happen to single guys in the history of mankind. In just a few short years, we have been given a tool that not only displays pictures of a girl, but also pictures of her friends, her relationship status, job and education info, and months' worth of wall posts from which invaluable data can been gleaned. We can ascertain what amounts to a full work-up on a chick before ever even meeting her. It's just like the individual Citysearch reviews I imagined—only better.

But as with any breakthrough in the game, there are hazards. The first thing to be wary of is the photos. These are obviously the reason men come to social networking sites to begin with, and it's also where guys and girls engage in information warfare. Women know what they're doing—they're standing sideways in every single picture, looking over their shoulder with shadows covering everything else. Hence it's called Facebook instead of Bodybook. Girls cleverly obscure themselves from the neck down because they know that the only thing guys need is one arm. I just need an unobstructed view of you from shoulder to elbow and I will extrapolate your entire body type in my mind—accurate or not. But women should be careful not to look *too* good in their profile pictures. You think I can't spot a glamour shot—otherwise known as the greatest posed picture of you ever taken? Sorry, but I'm moving on to the more extemporaneous album labeled "Wasted at Mardi Gras" instead. Ultimately, the key to a great Facebook profile is to look good without really trying—and without making me sift through five hundred pictures of your fucking sister's baby first.

GLOSSARY

KAROSPACING

Technique adopted by some of my buddies who troll through the thousands of fans on my Facebook, MySpace, Twitter, and Ruminations.com profiles looking for hot chicks to message. Surprisingly, it sometimes works; I've inadvertently created a secondary ass market for my friends.

An additional complication is the fact that most Facebook pictures have more than one person in them. How disappointing is it when you're stalking someone online and you finally find a picture that she's tagged in, but when you roll over the photo it turns out she's not the cute one? Very, very disappointing. Therefore, I think we should establish some rules. Ladies: posting a picture of yourself and a celebrity doesn't make you any more attractive. Guys: posting a picture of yourself and the one hot chick you happen to know from work doesn't make you less of a dork. Ladies: don't caption a photo of you and your girl friends as "my beautiful babies" when they're all busted. Guys: don't make your profile private; what are you, a chick? Ladies: don't list your age as 99 years old; now everyone just assumes you're older than thirty-five—be proud to be an Internet-savvy cougar!

Relationship status is another potential trap. Sometimes, women will put In a Relationship on their Facebook profile even though they're single, just so creepy guys won't hit on them. However, when you don't link to your boyfriend's name, or have even one picture of him in any of your photo albums, we're totally on to you. And please don't list your relationship status as Swinger, It's Complicated, or Married (to your best friend); just save us all the trouble and go with Single.

FURTHER ENRICHMENT

A less well-known place to ogle pictures of chicks online is law firm web sites. Most firms have high-quality, searchable headshots of all their nubile female associates. And usually next to the picture will be contact information and an option that says: "Download vCard." If only it were that easy.

While technology has helped me take my game to a whole new level, and allowed single people of both sexes to communicate with and stalk each other more freely than ever before, some of the problems that have always plagued us remain. For instance, when cell phones first became popular, I'd get a million accidental calls because my first name starts with two *A*s and is often listed first in friends' address books. Now, I get a million invitations to completely irrelevant events on Facebook—again because my first name is listed at the top and people are just clicking away indiscriminately. When I was a senior in college, my cell phone address book ran out of memory and every time I wanted to make room for a new number, I had to pick the contact I liked the least and delete him or her—kind of like cell phone *Survivor*. Then, last year, my Facebook account reached the 5,000-friend limit and now I can't add anyone else. It's the same issue all over again. Only now I have no idea how I'm gonna choose whom to defriend. Oh, who are we kidding? You know exactly how I'm gonna choose.

CLOSING TIME

When I've laid some groundwork, thwarted the HCIs, identified an eight or above on the classic scale, remembered her name, and vanquished the competition, it's time for the close. Scoring in cities where last call is late, such as New York, Chicago, or Miami, is less about attraction and more about attrition. "Magic Hour" occurs between 2:30 and 3:30 a.m. and refers to the window of time when girls are just drunk, tired, or lonely enough to respond to guys' advances. This is the perfect time to close because the girls who are left standing have essentially identified themselves as available for the taking. (Since bars close much earlier in LA, Magic Hour sadly does not exist here, and the entire process must be accelerated.) Regardless, the final dance has begun.

When I attempt to take a girl home from the bar against her better judgment, I need to have a retort handy for any excuse she could possibly give to not hook up with me, and just wear her down. "You have to get up really early tomorrow? No problem, I'll set an alarm." "You don't have your contact lens solution? We'll buy some on the way home. At least you're not wearing glasses." Sometimes a girl will attempt to dissuade me by managing expectations: "Listen, Karo, I'll go home with you, I guess, but I'm not gonna, like, do much. I just don't want you to be disappointed." Ladies, don't worry about me being disappointed. I went out looking for a nine and I'm going home with a six. That ship has sailed.

PREMATURE ELATION

One of the first rules of taking girls home from the bar is . . . actually take them home from the bar. One of my buddies was making out with this chick once when he decided the next logical move would be to try to take her pants off. When the girl stopped him, pointing out that they were indeed still at the bar, he uttered the classic response, "So?"

The thing is, when guys go out, we pretty much *need* to hook up. In case of a dry spell I have enough stock footage stored up to masturbate for six to ten weeks. But after that, sex is a biological requirement. When I approach that limit, I toss all my usual rules out the window and my motto becomes—to paraphrase the words of the esteemed sociologist 50 Cent—"Get Laid or Lie Tryin'." If I'm trying to take a girl home from a bar that's in kind of a sketchy neighborhood, but she's worried about leaving her friend behind, I'll continue to implore, "Come on, let's get outta here." And if my girl is like, "But ten dudes in biker jackets are hitting on my friend right now," I'll respond assuredly, "Don't worry, I'm sure she'll be fine."

Despite every element of my game firing on all cylinders, when I have a girl wrapped around my finger, there is usually only one thing that can prevent it from happening: her friend. Because every girl has that one friend who either lost her cell phone or can't find the other girls or got alcohol poisoning or has no place to stay. More potential sex has been squandered due to girls' friends than I care to quantify. Meanwhile, I'm muttering under my breath, "Fuck your friend; let's go!" But girls are loyal; they will not leave without their friend. And this is truly unacceptable. If I think there's even a *chance* I might be getting some ass, I take charge. "Listen up," I'll say. "Here's how we're gonna get your friend home." And then I lay out an overly elaborate plan designed to convince my target that her friend will be just fine going home with the bartender.

And when I've finally convinced a chick to go home with me, I don't take any chances—I leave *immediately*. I do not say goodbye to anyone. I'm like a phantom. Because I know that the longer my farewell lap, the greater the chance the girl is going to realize that this is a poor decision. I went to a party for a buddy of mine once and he introduced me to this really cute brunette. She wanted to go home with me, so I said, "Cool, let's bounce." Then she asked, "Don't you want to say goodbye to your friend first?" "Uh, not really." "But he's leaving to teach English in southeast Asia. You're not gonna see him for, like, two years." And I just wanted to say, "Darling, the best going-away present I could possibly give him is banging you."

SEALING THE DEAL

Once I've left the bar with a girl, there's no time to breathe easy. Although I may be only minutes away from sealing the deal, I'm not in the clear yet. My new number-one priorities become getting home as quickly as possible and keeping the girl occupied. I don't want her having any second thoughts about hooking up. If I'm in a cab with a girl and there's a lull in the conversation, I put on a fucking show. I sing and dance and shake my keys around, hoping a shiny object will distract her while I yell at the cabbie to *"Drive*—for the love of God, drive!"

I was in a cab home with this girl once, and everything was going great, and then the cab got into a huge head-on collision. No one was injured, thankfully, but the two cars were totaled and the girl was really shaken up. She said, "Oh my God. I can't believe that just happened. Can you take me home?" And I was like, "Of course. I mean, I thought that's what we were doing in the first place." And she said, "No, not like that. I mean can you help me *get* home. My head is spinning. Isn't yours?" And I wanted to reply, "Of course, a little. But my *cock* is fine." Instead, I said, "Yeah, I'm pretty freaked out too. I don't think either of us should be alone."

When I make it back to a girl's place, though, there is one situation that is an absolute worst-case scenario: if she has a pet. Not because I'm allergic, but because I fucking hate all animals. I'm sorry, but I don't care if it's a dog or a cat or a bird or a gerbil—get it out of my fucking face. It's not normal for people to have animals running around their house. It smells and it's gross and I don't give a shit what you named it after. And no, a cat isn't the cleanest animal there is — it shits in a fucking box in the kitchen! Get it away from me! I hate animals. I can barely stand humans.

TERMINOLOGY

"Co-opetition" is an economics term meaning cooperative competition. It comes into play when I bring a girl back to her apartment only to find that the girl's roommate has also brought a random dude home. Although this guy would represent my enemy at the bar, both men immediately recognize the need to work together in this situation and communicate a détente via wink or head nod. When the girls go to the kitchen or bathroom together, the two males dispense with pleasantries and get down to strategy. The guy handbook generally calls for some sort of pick play to be run where one guy distracts his girl long enough for the other guy to lure his girl into the bedroom. When implemented correctly, co-opetition can result in the highly desired "win-win situation."

Going back to my place involves a different set of obstacles and strategies. For instance, on more than one occasion I've brought a girl back to my apartment to drink wine only to discover that I have absolutely no idea how to open the bottle. And when at long last we finally make it into my bedroom, and everything is all set, I wait for the girl to go to the bathroom, then go into her purse and shut off her cell phone.

That way, later, when we're about to have sex and she says, "I wonder if my friend got home from the bar OK," I can just say, "Well, she never called so I'm sure everything is fine!"

There was a special time in my life when a very rare scenario occurred: I got laid early on a weekend night, like around 11 p.m., and then the girl left. When this happened, there was really only one thing I could do: shower up and head back out. I can't tell you what an exhilarating sensation it is to kick game knowing that you've already scored. There's no pressure; anything that happens is just a bonus. I felt invincible—like when you get the Starman in Mario Bros., except I didn't start blinking. I did, however, start thinking. If I were to hook up again, that'd be two girls, in one night, at separate times; that's unbelievable! Then I hit on every girl I saw, got shot down like Duck Hunt, and went home by myself before passing out while masturbating. Yup, I woke up in the morning with tissues stuck inside the waistband of my boxers like a Kleenex holster.

Some guys have complained to me that documenting stories like this, and in general revealing our tricks of the trade, both makes us look bad and destroys our competitive advantage. I disagree. On the contrary, I believe that the more informed a woman is, the more approachable she becomes. Besides, flirting really isn't about trickery or subterfuge. Chicks aren't stupid; they know what we're doing for the most part. It's all a carefully choreographed dance that girls choose to engage in willingly. After all, it takes two to play this game.

CHAPTER 3

THE NAKED TRUCE

Sex is a part of nature. I go along with nature.

MARILYN MONROE

One-night stands have traditionally been stigmatized as inappropriate sexual behavior. But as our generation gets married later and stays single longer, there are certain, well, needs that have to be met. Whether it's an inebriated, emotionless encounter or a longer-term, casual hookup, getting laid is no longer something to be ashamed of. In fact, when done with the right person (i.e., someone with more important things to do than worry about why you didn't call the next day, or month) sex is something to be proud of—a stress-relieving experience between two consenting adults and an endless source of barroom tales for a guy to share with his friends. For happily single men and women approaching thirty, hooking up is less about one party taking advantage of the other, and more about a mutual desire to blow off some steam. This tacit agreement to give in to our basest instincts while pledging to remain unattached is the naked truce. From late-night booty texts to morning-after escapades, the quest to lay pipe then escape unscathed occupies the majority of our time and energy. Is it worth it? Is mindless and often unsatisfying sex better than no sex at all? Single people ponder these dilemmas with each other, though often the answer to these questions is simply another question: "Wanna get out of here?"

GREAT EXPECTATIONS

Since time immemorial, the phrase "Let's go back to my place and watch a movie" has been code for "Let's have sex within the next forty to fifty minutes." To this day, my Netflix account is simply a list of films I've only seen half of. My pants come off and I'm like, "OK, send this one back to the top of the queue!" The first time a girl goes home with a guy, she'll often try to be stern and lay down the law as to how far the hook-up is gonna go. One of my all-time favorite scenarios occurs when I've been hitting on a girl all night and throwing every piece of game I have at her. When I finally get her home, and we start hooking up, she pauses, looks at me, and whispers, "Just so you know, I'm not sleeping with you." But instead of being dejected, I'm elated because now I know at least I'm getting a blow job.

When a guy and girl are casually hooking up, it is expected that each encounter should build on the previous one. If you let me dabble in your pants last time, I expect you to dabble in mine this time. One of the most confusing situations for a guy is when a girl who has previously gone down on him will now barely touch him. Our brains cannot process this reversal of fortune. The whole reason I called you was because I knew that, even in the worst-case scenario, I'd at least be getting head. Now you're saying I should take you to dinner? I'm not following.

This same line of reasoning can be applied to sex once the relationship has made it that far. It's all about momentum. The first go-round you often stick to standard missionary. The second time, girl-on-top gets thrown into the mix. The third stint introduces doggie, and so forth. Eventually you start anticipating your partner's moves to the point where it almost becomes boring. This is called "marriage."

FUN FACT

If a man takes a woman's virginity, or gives her her first orgasm, he is entitled to sleep with her for the rest of his life.

The go-to excuse for women who want to put the brakes on a hook-up is, of course, menstruation. It's like Kryptonite to my penis. A lot has been said about women faking orgasms. Eh, I'm not that impressed. To me, a woman's true power lies in her ability to fake a period. If a girl wants to stop me dead in my tracks, all she has to do is say the *word* "period." Plus, chicks can use the same excuse over and over again because we're never going to call them out on it. I had a girl pull the

P-card on me twice only three weeks apart. I started to think that either she didn't want to sleep with me or I didn't pay very good attention in high school health class.

BE PREPARED

For bachelors, preparedness begins at home. Impeccable personal hygiene is a must to ensure success with the ladies. Which is why I always trim downstairs. This area needs to be as well-groomed and welcoming as possible. In fact, I shave my boys with the same buzzer I use to shave my face. I'm not sure why women shudder when I admit this. What's the big deal? Those are the two cleanest parts of my body. Personal grooming is a two-way street, however. Ladies, I don't care what you read in *Cosmo* or saw on *Sex and the City*. When in doubt, trim. This is what sophisticated, single men prefer. I have never, ever heard a guy complain to me that a girl he hooked up with had too *little* hair down there. This ain't 1968.

Music is another key component to a proper naked pow-wow—not only because it sets the mood but also because it muffles moans and thus discourages inhibition. Even if it's not the music you listen to on a daily basis, skilled bachelors maintain dedicated playlists for the right occasions—set to shuffle and repeat all. For instance, I mostly listen to hip hop and Top 40, but the two most-played artists on my iTunes are Jack Johnson and John Legend. And I've never listened to either of them alone, clothed, or sober.

MOOD MUSIC

Here are some actual albums from my iTunes library to serve as examples of what to play and what not to play when entertaining a woman in bed.

YES

John Legend, *Once Again*

Jack Johnson, *Brushfire Fairytales*

Bob Marley, *Legend*

Common, *Like Water for Chocolate*

NO!

Snoop Dogg, *Doggystyle*

Rage Against the Machine, *Evil Empire*

DMX, *It's Dark and Hell Is Hot*

Avenue Q, *Original Broadway Cast Soundtrack*

If I'm on tour or on vacation, I still remain diligent. I've learned that I often lose my hotel key, and the time it takes to request a replacement is ample time for a girl to get cold feet. When I check in, I always request a second key and leave it in an envelope at the front desk for a "friend" — that friend being drunk me five hours later. Also, though it seems counterintuitive, a suite or luxurious room is not always the best bet. Oftentimes I simply request the smallest room with one big bed. I call it the "nowhere to go but bang" option.

My personal favorite move is to go to the bathroom as soon as we get back to my place, take off my belt, and hide it in the bathtub. In my entire history of being sexually active, no girl has ever picked up on it. The brilliance of this is that it helps eliminate barriers to entry. If a girl is contemplating touching my junk, I don't want any possible roadblocks standing in her way, belt included.

PROTECTION

Recently I was using the unisex bathroom in an office building when I noticed there was a twenty-five-cent tampon dispenser on the wall. Fair enough—chicks need that shit. But right next to it was a twenty-five-cent condom dispenser. I mean, I guess you can argue that both tampons and condoms can be needed in an emergency. But that really all depends on your definition of "emergency."

Condoms are a very necessary evil, and I carry them whenever I leave the house after dusk. Discretion is always paramount, however. For instance, if I take a girl home from the bar, even if we go back to *her* place, it's expected that *I'll* have a condom. What respectable single guy wouldn't? But it's best not to reveal how respectable you are too soon. I was once at a cocktail party, hitting on the chick sitting next to me on the sofa. When I went to grab my phone out of my pocket, a condom fell out too. The girl looked at me with such disdain as the condom just sat between us for a moment, taunting me. I had little use for it that night.

SHOPPING GUIDE

Purchasing condoms is embarrassing enough without having to stand there reading each label. For years, I've tried to find a type that actually felt somewhat enjoyable, which inevitably means experimenting with ones that are less effective. First I tried extra strength, but I didn't like those, so then I tried extra sensitive, then ultra comfort, ultimate feeling, enhanced pleasure, high sensation, extra thin, ultra thin, and finally ones that I'm pretty sure came with a warning on the package that read: "Not for use with vagina."

I was going through security at LAX once and a TSA worker was reminding travelers to remove all coins, keys, and credit cards from their pockets. When it was my turn, the guy repeated his mantra, only this time he said, "Please remove all coins, keys, credit cards, and condoms from your pockets." I did a double take. First of all, can condoms actually set off the metal detector? Second of all—and more importantly—do I just *look* like the kind of dude who carries condoms onto an airplane? Granted, that was the look I was going for, but I didn't think I could pull it off. It was like being put on a watch list for the mile-high club.

Despite the bother of choosing, buying, and carrying condoms, I always practice safe sex. But I still hate it. I lose all sensation. I put a condom on and all of a sudden I'm in that Gatorade commercial. I'm like, "Is it in you?" And there's nothing worse than *thinking* I'm fucking, only to look down to see that I'm actually penetrating the space between the girl's ass and the mattress. Sometimes it just happens. I can't tell, especially if they're nice sheets. When I hook up with a girl and the next day my friend asks me how the sex was, I brag, "The thread count was fantastic."

CLOTHES ENCOUNTERS

My buddy went home with this girl once, and when he tried to take her pants off, she said, "No, wait, you can't. It's a long story." Ladies, if you don't want us to take your pants off, don't say "long story." Believe me, you don't want to let guys' imaginations run wild. When my buddy told me what happened, I said to him, matter-of-factly, "Well, obviously she has a cock." He started freaking out. I was like, "What other explanation could there be? Long story short, she has a penis."

I've always hated getting naked with a girl. I love *being* naked with a girl, just not the effort it takes to get there. First of all, I'm embarrassed to admit that I've never taken off a bra with one hand. Sorry, can't do it. I've actually watched several YouTube videos on the subject. I still have no idea. If that wasn't bad enough, these skinny jeans are now all the rage. They are the bane of my existence. They are impossible to get off without one, if not both participants breaking a sweat. What I'd like to see next season is girls' jeans that rip off like basketball warm-ups. But I'll settle for boot cut.

Nothing is more disappointing to me than seeing a girl's thong on the floor. It's just so insubstantial—I feel like I worked so hard to get that sucker off and what does it do as soon as it hits the floor? Curl up in a little ball like it's frightened. It looks like one of those Shrinky Dinks we used to put in the oven when we were kids. A thong on the floor blends in and disappears like camouflage. The girl asks me if I see her underwear anywhere and I say, "I can't find it. All I see is this candy wrapper." She's like, "No, that's it."

GLOSSARY

SB (PRONOUNCED "SIB")

SB is short for "surprise body." A SB is a girl who, when you remove her bulky clothing while hooking up, turns out to have an amazing figure. There's nothing like taking that J.Crew rollneck off to discover a six-pack and two cannons beneath all that wool. Unfortunately, SBs are very rarely found in the wild, but are more prevalent in frigid, mountainous states and at North Face headquarters.

When I moved from New York to Los Angeles, I joked that I was coming to LA to further my comedy career and for the opportunity to touch fake breasts for the first time. Maybe I'm naïve, but to me, fake breasts fall into that same category as strange piercings and tattoos—if a girl's got 'em, clearly she likes to get down. I mean, no chick with an eyebrow ring has ever said, "You can't take my pants off. It's a long story." When I finally did touch my first pair of fake breasts, I was kind of disappointed. They were, like, little Cs. If you're gonna get fake breasts, you should be walking around with weapons of mass destruction. Fuck little Cs, you should have triple Zs. Your breasts should be so big you're living in the bell tower at Notre Dame, that's how much of a hunchback you are.

I once hooked up with a girl who had her own eyes tattooed on the middle of her back. That's right—the tattoo artist sketched her eyes, and then made a tattoo of them. But it wasn't a tramp stamp—you could only see the tattoo if she was topless and had her back to you. I like to believe this girl got the tattoo for the sole purpose of creating the illusion that you're looking into her eyes while banging her from behind—which of course defeats the whole purpose of doggie style.

HOOKED UP

Another flaw in my arsenal is that I'm not really good at hooking up . . . sober. It just happens so rarely that I never get any practice. Unless I'm in a serious relationship, I can't really imagine a scenario where I *would* be hooking up without having a few drinks first. When I'm sober, I get too far inside my head and start to overthink things I'd never even consider if I was wasted. My inner monologue is like, "Hmm . . . should I lick her nipple? I don't know. Do people even lick nipples anymore? Yeah, I'm thinking that should be my next move. Oh man, I could really use a tequila shot."

I think if sex were a sport my scouting report would say that my biggest weakness is spooning. I've never really mastered the technique. Why am I on my side? I feel so out of place. By thirty I thought I would have addressed all the holes in my game. Instead I'm completely worthless unless the girl is braless, I'm wasted, and there's no spooning involved.

MAILBAG

One of the questions I get most frequently from my female readers is, "What are guys thinking about during sex? Is he thinking about me? Is he thinking about Jessica Alba? Is he thinking about his fantasy football team? What's the deal?" Well, if we're talking about a one-night stand, surprisingly the answer is none of the above. Usually I'm thinking, "Oh man, I can't believe I'm actually having sex right now—this is awesome! I'm so happy I decided to go out tonight! Dude, in ninth grade, did you ever actually think you'd be having semi-regular sex? I don't think so! This is *so* cool!" I guess the novelty just never wears off.

I've recently been informed that I text incorrectly because I use my right thumb and left index finger instead of both thumbs, which is apparently how the rest of the world does it. Normally I wouldn't be too concerned, but about five years ago, I found out that I also snap incorrectly (I use my thumb and index finger instead of thumb and middle finger). Now I can't stop thinking about why the fuck I can't use my fingers properly and—gasp!—what else I may have been doing wrong the whole time.

The benefit of hooking up drunk is that it renders all these deficiencies moot because both parties are sloppy, uninhibited, and won't remember much in the morning anyway. Plus, there's the fight-or-flight factor. When I hook up drunk I find myself attempting positions my body normally wouldn't be able to handle. It's kind of like if you witness an accident and then run over and lift an entire car off a person because your adrenaline is pumping so hard. No one has ever had sex standing, hanging, or balancing unless they're hammered.

OBSERVATION

Getting laid while wasted can be a tricky endeavor. Sometimes it just doesn't work. If I'm too fucked up, trying to have sex is like trying to get the straw into a Capri Sun.

Have you ever been hooking up and realized the other person is still chewing gum? And she's not even chewing it, but rather just holding it in her mouth like a wad of tobacco. What possible reason could a girl have to chew gum while hooking up? If she's worried about her breath, a two-hour-old piece of Orbit ain't gonna help. When I call a girl out on it, she gets slightly embarrassed and offers to get up and throw it out. Not so fast—once I've got you in bed and horizontal, I'm not taking any chances. One time I asked a girl if she could just swallow her gum. She responded, "Oh, I don't swallow." Well, that sucks for me.

Whenever I'm trying to sleep with a girl, I always keep one hand on her body at all times. It's kind of like one of those contests where whoever touches the car the longest wins it. If I go to shut off the light, I keep a hand on her breast. Looking for a condom? Hand on her ass. Just like all my other strategies, it's all about keeping her preoccupied. I may not be able to take her bra off, but I sure can put a condom on while making out and never break stride.

One of my least favorite sexual situations is hooking up in a pitch-black room with a chick who doesn't make any sound. I have no idea what's going on. I think to myself, "Is she enjoying this? Am I hurting her? For God's sake, gimme a whimper or something." Then my eyes start to adjust and I hear this strange noise and I'm like, "Wait a minute. Where did you get another piece of gum?"

DIRTY TALK

The girls I hook up with these days are comfortable with their bodies, they know what they like, and they're vocal about it. Which is good. But the thing is, if a girl tells me what gets her off, pretty much no matter what it is, I'll do it. If the girl says, "I want you to kiss my neck—but not too hard—then do a triple lutz off the bed, come back, and punch me in the face," I'll reply, "Not a problem." But when I tell a girl what I like, she treats it like a negotiation. I'll say, "Actually, I really like it when you kiss my nipples." And she'll respond, "Let me think about that. No. What else ya got?"

I can talk dirty if I need to; I can keep up. But is there anything more awkward than when you talk dirty and the girl doesn't hear you the first time? The girl will be moaning, "Oh, Karo. Oh yeah. That's good." And I'll whisper, "Oh yeah, I love your ass." And she's like, "What?" I'm completely embarrassed. "Um. I love your . . . ass? I don't know, it sounded better the first time."

The worst is when the girl says something that makes me realize she's totally not paying attention. We're going at it, I've got my iTunes hook-up playlist rocking, everything's great, and I whisper, "Does that feel good?" And she's like, "Oh my God . . . I love this song." Really? Well then go fuck John Legend!

OBSERVATION

Ever notice that when you're hooking up and the other person says, "Oh right there," or "Just like that," you immediately forget what the hell you were doing and totally fuck it up? I think to myself, "Wait, what was I doing? Was it like this? I lost my rhythm now. What was my cadence again?"

When I'm hooking up with a particular girl for the first time, I love the pillow talk chess match that goes on. If she says, "Karo, I've actually never gone down on a guy before," I'll call her bluff and respond reassuringly, "It's OK. I'll teach you." If she says, "Karo, I just got out of a serious relationship," I'll reply, "It's OK. I'll be your rebound guy." If the girl is really into it, and she begs, "Karo, you can do anything you want to me," I'll always pause, consider the request, and then ask, "Anal?" To which the inevitable response is, "Anything but that."

I'm convinced that twice as many girls have experimented with anal sex as actually admit it. The scenario is always the same: you were with your boyfriend, he kept begging you, you had a little too much wine and, well, it *was* his birthday. Then he stuck it in a quarter of an inch, it was excruciatingly pain-ful, and you vowed never to do it again. Hey, can't blame you for trying.

The ultimate form of dirty talk is, of course, phone sex. It can get confusing, however, especially when practicing safe sex with a girl in real life, and then occasionally having phone sex with her to boot. The girl will say on the phone, "Karo, I want you to fuck me right here and right now." And I'll lean into the phone and whisper, "I'm kissing your neck, I'm strok-ing the inside of your thigh . . . and now I'm running across the street to buy condoms at the gas station."

GETTING A HEAD

At times, being a single guy feels like a grind. We have to work so hard to hook up. Which is why it's disheartening that fellatio is more commonly known as "giving head." This im-plies that a blow job is a gift that any guy should be apprecia-tive of ever receiving. Sadly, it's true: we have very little say in the matter. But that doesn't dissuade us from pursuing BJs with unparalleled intensity.

Many people believe that fellatio is a more intimate act than sex. I don't disagree. After all, a girl can tell if she really likes a guy by the way she feels when she's around him, or if she gets goose bumps when he kisses her. I know that I really have feelings for a girl when I feel bad that she's blowing me. As I've already made clear, my boys are well-groomed and immaculate. But any guy who spends hours in a hot, crowded bar and then goes home to hook up has the equivalent of five jeans manufacturing plants in his boxers—that's how much of a sweatshop it is down there.

> ### GLOSSARY
>
> #### THE FRIGHTENED PELICAN
> Ladies, I have a request: spit or swallow, but choose *one*. Sometimes I'll be getting head and, as I'm coming to fruition, the girl will hesitate, call an audible, get some in her mouth, and have no idea what to do with it. She then proceeds to stagger wide-eyed across the room, chin out, arms flailing wildly, searching for a place to spit. This, my friends, is called the frightened pelican.

Giving and receiving head has its share of awkward moments. Like when you randomly make eye contact with the girl while she's in the act. She always has that deer-in-headlights look on her face. And there's nothing more uncomfortable than never-ending head. Whether it's because I'm drunk or she's using teeth, blow jobs really only have an enjoyable shelf life of about ten minutes max. After that, there's just something disconcerting about a girl sighing while my penis is in her mouth.

Luckily, when the going is slow, guys have an easily accessible erogenous zone: our balls. Girls should learn to caress and befriend them. Experienced women will pay more attention there than anywhere else. Believe me, it definitely speeds up the process. Just don't be *too* enthusiastic. A buddy of mine once told me he took home a girl from a bar and got head so incredible that in the middle he actually became concerned. Not that he might finish too quickly, but that the girl he was with could be a paid professional.

PRODUCE THE GIRL

Sex isn't so amazing just because it's pleasurable, it's so amazing because it only happens when all of a bachelor's hard-earned work finally pays off. Sometimes it's more of a relief than anything. All that drinking, all that flirting, all that rejection wasn't pointless after all. But once I find a partner who's willing and able, the fun has only just begun. For instance, I was hooking up with this chick once, and she wanted me to lift her up and fuck her on her desk. And I was like, "Not a problem." But there *was* a problem, namely the desk was a little too high. So I'm holding her up and we're going at it, but it's totally awkward and I'm standing on my tippy toes, and then all of a sudden she yells, "Wait, wait, stop!" I thought she was having second thoughts. Instead she just wanted me to move over because my balls were on her 401(k) paperwork. That's the kind of shit that never happened when I was twenty.

PUBLIC SERVICE ANNOUNCEMENT

Attention women: The penis, as you are well aware, is a very sensitive organ. If we are having sexual intercourse, and you are on top, "riding me," as it were, please do not rapidly hop up and down on said organ like a fucking bunny rabbit. It's not a toy. Do not mistake me grabbing your shoulders as a sign that I'm enjoying it. I'm merely trying to hold you down so that you don't fly off and break my dick in half.

One of the first girls I slept with after moving to Los Angeles was also the loudest. To say she was a screamer would be an understatement. About twenty minutes into our roll in the hay, my doorbell rang. My first thought was, "Wait, I have a doorbell?" But I quieted the chick down and got up to look through the peephole, where I spied the building's security guard. I opened the door and this bleary-eyed dude with a faded blue uniform said to me, "I'm sorry to bother you, sir, but we received a noise complaint. However, in order to validate the complaint, I stood outside your door for five minutes listening." I gulped hard as the guard continued. "At first I heard screaming and moaning," he said, "but then I just heard screaming." And then, I shit you not, he uttered to me the following words: "Produce the girl, sir."

Stunned, I said to the guy, "Wait a minute. You think I'm beating her?" He just repeated: "Produce the girl, sir." I said, "Come on, man. We had a few drinks, we're just having some fun." "Produce the girl, sir," he said once again as he reached for some kind of nightstick or Taser he had on his belt. "Whoa, whoa, no need for that," I pleaded. "We're all friends here. Just give me a second." So I ran into the bedroom, got this sloppy drunk chick out of bed, threw some clothes on her, and brought her out to inform the nice security guard that I was not in fact beating her. When the guy was sufficiently convinced, he apologized for disturbing us, asked me to keep it down, and informed me that I would be receiving a $500 fine from building management. So I went back in the bedroom and got my money's worth.

COME AS YOU ARE

Guys like to look at their bedside alarm clock just before sex and time how long we can last. Along with rating girls, this is just another example of guys bringing their love of stats and competition into the bedroom. But no matter what happens, sex always seems to go a lot quicker than I expected. At the end, I think, "Damn, that took forever; must be a new record!" And then I look at the clock and exclaim, "Seven minutes!?"

I've realized that, believe it or not, many women have a stronger sex drive than I do. I slept with this chick once, and about a minute after we finished, she turned to me and said, "Karo, let's see how many times we can fuck tonight." And I was like, "Actually, I think I'm good." I don't know why women are obsessed with having sex more than once in a night. Listen, everybody loves orgasms, but for women, the more the merrier. For guys, there's a law of diminishing returns.

I really don't understand the point of the much-lauded simultaneous orgasm. Can't I just have my own orgasm? You're getting a whole bunch; I only get one. If you don't mind, I'd like to enjoy mine without worrying about getting you off at the exact same time. You see, guys *give* girls orgasms. It's a manual procedure. One hand here, one hand there, medium thrust, and . . . we have liftoff. But girls don't give guys orgasms. The male orgasm is like flying on autopilot. No matter what she does, I'm gonna get where I'm going eventually.

Ultimately, for women, sex is really all in their heads. I'll be sleeping with a girl, and she'll whisper, "Karo, I had a really stressful day at work. The market was way down. I'm just not gonna be able to have an orgasm." And I'll say, "I had a pretty tough day too. Turns out Uncle Frank has cancer. It's terminal. So . . . a little to the left? Uncle Frank would have wanted it this way."

ETIQUETTE

Instead of smoking a cigarette after sex, I check my BlackBerry. It doesn't smell bad, it won't cause cancer, but it has the same soothing effect.

You know the sex was great when you open your eyes and you've forgotten where you are for a moment; like you've gone back in time. I have to stop myself from muttering, "What year is it?" Now the good part about sex is that it's awesome. The bad part about sex is that it's messy. In movies, sex always ends with some sort of dramatic flourish, and the couple float gracefully into each other's arms. In real life, sex ends with a grunt and then a frantic search for the forty requisite tissues. Of course, the box of Kleenex is always *just* out of reach, like in *Indiana Jones and the Last Crusade* when he can only get a fingertip on the Holy Grail. If no tissues are available, I'm usually instructed to roll clear while the girl disengages and makes a mad dash to the bathroom. Of course, all of this is done in part to prevent the sheets from getting dirty. The very sheets, ironically enough, that not seven minutes ago I was fucking vigorously.

TALES OF WHOA

If I'm hooking up with a girl who's previously hooked up with one of my friends, sometimes she'll ask, "Karo, you swear you won't tell Evan about this?" I always promise to oblige, then immediately resume struggling with her skinny jeans. Of course, the first thing I do upon leaving the scene is call the guy friend in question and tell him every detail—including the fact that the girl asked me not to, which is often the best part of the story.

When a man is telling his friends that he slept with a woman, there's one phrase that he'll usually use. He'll say, "I fucked the shit out of her." Not "I slept with her," "We had sex," or "We made love." No, it's "I fucked the shit out of her." We are not deterred from using this phrase, despite the fact that it is very rarely true. I could go home with a girl, not be able to get it up, and then prematurely ejaculate, and the next day I'd still be like, "Yo, I fucked the shit out of her! I'm the man!"

GLOSSARY

THE CODE OF AFS

AFS stands for "Anything For a Story." All guys operate implicitly under the Code of AFS, which requires them, while hooking up, to try to do something weird or outrageous—like get down in a public place or stick a finger where it doesn't belong—just so they can tell their friends about it later. Nothing whips a pack of males into a frenzy faster than hearing a compatriot's hilarious tale of debauchery. The dirtier and more outlandish, the better.

Even if a guy promises a girl he "won't say anything about what happened," it's a sure bet that the story will spread to his friends faster than at breakfast the morning after a frat party. After all, there's nothing like passing up an intimate and gratifying love-making experience just for the opportunity to be the man of the hour during the next guys' night out. Oftentimes during sex, instead of thinking, "How can I pleasure this woman?" I'm thinking, "I can't believe she agreed to do it in the hallway. And I don't even live in this building! The boys are gonna love this . . ."

I would venture to say that I derive more pleasure from telling and retelling a good, crazy, wasted hook-up story than from the experience itself. I don't even think I need the actual hook-up, just the memory of it. Like the plot of the movie *Total Recall* but with blow jobs. Every guy treats his history of one-night stands differently. My friend Moobs (so nick-named because of his prominent man-boobs) always carries a digital camera and has a picture of every girl he's ever hooked up with. Looking at his Facebook albums is like flipping through the women's section of an old Banana Republic cata-log, except you know all the clothes ended up on the floor. My surgeon buddy Shermdog, whose prowess is the stuff of legend, maintains a cordial relationship with virtually all of his hook-ups, and I believe checks in with each of them on a biannual basis. That's what I call bedside manner.

Occasionally, I'm fortunate enough to be a part of the story even though I wasn't part of the action. For instance, in 2006 I was sailing with some friends along the Great Barrier Reef. The tour got interesting one night when I awoke to find an Aussie chick climbing into bed with me on the deck of the ship, clearly wanting to hook up. In my drunken/sleeping haze, it took me a few minutes to realize she thought I was my buddy Mike. Noticing she had already removed her bra (how did she know my weakness?) and fearing an international in-cident, I hesitantly told her that I was not, in fact, Mike. In-credibly embarrassed, she flitted away, crying, "All you Amer-icans look the same!"

I think that tales of one-night stands are the universal lan-guage of twentysomething and thirtysomething males. Put two random dudes in a room together and eventually they'll start swapping war stories from the previous weekend's conquests. When we grow older, get married, and have kids, we lose that common bond. That's why golf is so popular. Put my dad in a room with some other old guy, and eventually they'll start swapping war stories from the previous weekend's back nine. The thing is, I don't play golf. So I guess the best excuse I have to continue sleeping around is that I still want to be able to relate to my friends without picking up a five iron.

DOWN FOR THE COUNT

Sometimes, I'll be hooking up with a girl, about to sleep with her, and she'll all of a sudden get concerned that I "get around" too much. "Karo," she'll ask, "how many girls have you slept with?" And I respond, "To be honest, I don't really count." But she'll persist, asking, "Well, is it at least, like, less than a hundred?" "A hundred!?" I'll grimace. "Is that your standard for sleeping with a guy? I don't know if *I* want to fuck *you* now!"

Of course, I do count. We all do. I may not know all their names, but I do know how many there have been. Yes, it's crude. Yes, it's immature. Yes, I probably shouldn't have bet my buddy Claudio who could sleep with the most girls by Thanksgiving one year. The fact is, I'm a thirty-year-old dude. My days of organized athletics are over. I don't have time for fantasy sports. This is all I've got. Besides, no one gets hurt (except for Claudio, who still owes me fifty bucks).

GLOSSARY

THE HOOK-UP CYCLE

Derived from the baseball term "hitting for the cycle," in which a player hits a single, double, triple, and home run in the same game. Hitting for the hook-up cycle means hooking up with a freshman, sophomore, junior, and senior in the same week in college. Ironically, the closest I ever came was after I had already graduated from Penn, during my first visit back for homecoming. Alas, I fell one junior girl short.

Even if it's only for his own personal gratification, a man takes great pride in how high his "number" is. Which is why, in my running lifetime tally of how many girls I've slept with, I've begun to include fractions. Like if a girl wants to have sex but I'm just too fucked up and can only infiltrate the outlying regions, that's two-thirds. If I fuck the mattress for ten minutes by accident, that's a half. Count it! My buddies will ask, "Hey Karo, did you get laid on vacation?" And I'm like, "Hell yeah, two and an eighth girls!"

When a guy isn't sure if what he did the previous night should count as getting laid, the next morning he'll convene a tribunal of his friends to analyze the evidence. Think of it as The Hague of drunken sex. Both sides of the case will be argued and the man in question will be ridiculed incessantly for not sealing the deal beyond a shadow of a doubt. The tribunal is quite forgiving, however, and will generally award a point (or fraction of a point, as the case may be) as long as "yes" is the answer to the question "Was there intent to penetrate?"

THE DOUBLE STANDARD

It is without question that men and women are judged by different standards. If a girl sleeps around, she is called a slut. If a guy sleeps around, he gets a book deal. Even so, women should be cognizant of the double standard and take some measures to protect their reputation. You don't want to end up like my ex-girlfriend's best friend. This chick was always growing out the front of her hair and it looked ridiculous. So I gave her a nickname: Bangs. The name worked on two levels because she also fucked everything that moved. Get it? Bangs. I thought it was brilliant. My ex-girlfriend? Not so much.

There are a few surefire ways for a guy to determine whether the girl he's with gets around. For instance, if I'm hooking up with a girl and, when she takes off her jeans, she takes off her thong at the same time, that's a big red flag. Listen, even if you're gonna sleep with me anyway, at least go through the motions of acting like you don't do this every night. Don't get me wrong, I appreciate the enthusiasm—but I'd feel a lot more comfortable if we stuck to the usual two-step process.

OBSERVATION

I've found that girls who don't have a lot of female friends tend to be wilder in bed. I believe this is because girls tell their friends all the gritty details the day after they get laid—and their friends (admittedly or not) then pass judgment on them. But girls without female friends are less inhibited about one-night stands because they don't have to worry about being judged by their peers. These girls answer to a higher authority. Sort of like the Hebrew National of hook-ups.

Believe it or not, there are actually certain instances when being labeled a slut can be a positive thing. For instance, let's say I tell a friend that I just met a girl on line at the grocery store and we totally hit it off. If my friend says, "Dude, I know that girl. She's a total whore," I'll be really disappointed. But if I'm wasted at the bar and I tell my friend I just met a girl on line for the bathroom and we totally hit it off, and my friend tells me she's a total whore, I'm thrilled.

I love when I run into a slutty girl I haven't seen in a while, and she introduces me to her new boyfriend. I'm like, "Oh, hey Melissa." And she says, "Karo, I want you to meet my boyfriend, Jack." I shake Jack's hand and tell him it's nice to meet him, but I also chuckle discreetly and think about whether or not he knows his girlfriend slept with . . . everybody.

LAY OVER

One of the most important keys to a successful one-night stand is having an exit strategy. First of all, no one wants to sleep next to a random person. I don't even want to sleep next to someone I like. There's only room for three arms to be resting comfortably in bed, and the fourth never has any place to go. I believe one-night stands are like rescuing someone from a burning building. You want to get in and out as quickly as possible, and then, maybe, you call a few days later to make sure everyone's OK. If you're at someone else's place, you need to leave as soon as you open your eyes. Breakfast? You gotta be kidding me. You'll be lucky if you get a wall post. And if you leave now maybe I won't even Twitter about it.

In my bedroom in LA, my bed is purposely set eight to ten inches away from the wall. This allows me to sleep undisturbed while the girl makes a quick and easy exit in the morning. And by "sleep undisturbed" I mean pretend to be passed out until she leaves and I can finally take a shit. But in an effort to heed my own advice, when I'm at a girl's place, sometimes I overcompensate and leave too early. I'll go to the bathroom right after sex and never come back. I've been told this is offensive.

GLOSSARY

SEXUAL LOITERING

When last night's conquest does not leave promptly the next morning. Should be illegal.

I once hooked up with a girl at my place and the next morning we exchanged pleasantries and got dressed. But she didn't leave. I actually left her in my apartment, went out and ran errands, then came back and she was still there. I turned the heat up all the way and tried to sweat her out. Nothing. I started to concoct arduous tasks that I needed to do that day in order to try to get rid of her ("Um, I really need to wash the windows"). She offered to help. I jumped in the shower. She joined me, uninvited. I peed in the shower, she didn't care. She would not leave. I was seriously thinking about calling the cops to remove her. I was wasted the night before. Who knows? I could have taken home a well-dressed homeless chick. She finally left around 7:30 p.m. It was a one-*day* stand.

What I've never understood is why girls are always so self-conscious about getting dressed the morning after. We've been naked hooking up all night and now you're trying to put your thong back on without lifting your ass from the bed? You're so adamant about not letting me see your breasts again that you're desperately trying to wiggle back into your bra without taking your shirt off first? And it's such a struggle too. I've watched chicks almost dislocate their own shoulders like Mel Gibson in *Lethal Weapon 2*. Why didn't you pull that kinky shit when we were hooking up?

Another question I often get from my female readers is "Why didn't he call?" Ladies, if you hook up with a guy and then he never calls you, there are really only a few possible reasons: one, he was already seeing someone else and that relationship has since gotten more serious; two, you're not nearly as cute in person as you look on Facebook; three, you didn't fuck him; or four, you did fuck him. I realize those last two are confusing, but those are the facts of life when dealing with a swinging bachelor. The phrase "I'll call you later" can either mean "I'll hit you up in a few hours" or "I'll talk to you when we awkwardly bump into each other in a few months and I try desperately not to make it seem obvious that I'm racking my brain to remember who the fuck you are."

LOST AND FOUND

Why do chicks always leave something at my place? Thongs I understand. They're fucking invisible. But why can't girls remember that they were wearing those big J.Lo hoop earrings that went out of style five years ago? They're right on my nightstand. And when the girl inevitably texts me to get her belongings back, I often outsource the dirty work to my doorman. I tell the girl I'm going on vacation for one to seven weeks and that she can pick up her stuff whenever. Then I give the doorman an unmarked package and tell him to give it to the first girl who inquires. I'd write her name on it, but I'm not sure if it's spelled with two *L*s, or is Stacey.

I never lose an article of clothing at a girl's place. When I get dressed to go out on a Saturday night, I think of the ensemble I've put together as one would of his fellow marines—leave no man behind. Besides, I need that light-blue T-shirt. I only have seven T-shirts. I lose one, that fucks up the rotation. If we're at her place, when we get naked I always stack my possessions in an orderly fashion on the floor. Socks go into my Cons, followed by wallet in the left sneaker, watch and BlackBerry in the right, and T-shirt stuffed into jeans. (I also don't pull the hide-the-belt trick and leave it safely in its loops.) If I realize at dawn that I've suffered from a severe case of beer goggles, this tidy arrangement allows me to quickly scoop up my shit, run into the hallway in my boxers, and get dressed in the elevator.

AMBITIOUS IDEAS

I've been thinking a lot lately about giving back to the community, and I've come up with an innovative proposal. What I'd like to do is open a thrift store—to benefit charity—that's stocked with the clothing and accessories that chicks leave in guys' apartments and never claim. There would be an entire section full of wife-beaters. It would be glorious.

I'd also like to invent some sort of one-night-stand pre-nup. Like in exchange for promising to call you within a week, you can't talk shit about me to your friends. Or in exchange for arranging the expedient return of all articles of clothing you leave behind, you promise not to steal the sweatpants I give you for the walk home. It's pretty ingenious. Now if only I could get a girl to sign it while wasted in the back of a cab on the way to my place.

Claudio once got so drunk that he hooked up with a girl, the next day she was gone, and he couldn't remember anything. So we're trying to figure out what the hell happened, and he finds this lone flip-flop that she must have somehow left underneath his bed. We were staring at it, and finally I said, "Dude, who leaves behind one shoe? I think you might have fucked Cinderella." Now you may scoff at the idea of fucking Cinderella, but believe it or not, I banged Sleeping Beauty. I'm not kidding. I was on tour in Orlando, I met this girl after a show, and her actual day job was playing Sleeping Beauty at Disney World. So we hooked up, and the next morning I checked out of my hotel and left her passed out in the bed. I figured she was used to it.

THE LONGEST WALK OF SHAME

One year, I was on tour in Arizona and I woke up the morning after a show in some random chick's bed. My first thought was, "I gotta get the hell out of here!" So I popped out of bed, grabbed my wallet and cell phone, tiptoed down the stairs, got dressed, busted out the front door, ran onto the sidewalk, and realized . . . where the fuck am I? I was on a tree-lined street in the suburbs of Tucson. There were no cabs and no one around. I had no clue where I was. I was officially lost on the walk of shame.

Just as I was trying to figure out my next move, my phone rang. It was one of my buddies in New York. It was 9 a.m. there; he was already in the office and was just calling to leave a message asking how the show went. I seized the opportunity. "Dude," I pleaded, "you gotta help me! I hooked up with this chick and now I'm lost in the middle of Tucson." I paused, looked around, noticed a street sign, then exclaimed, "Google Map this address!"

Soon my friend had pinpointed my location on Google Earth and, scanning the area, noticed a hospital about six blocks north by northwest of my position. I knew I could get a cab at the hospital, so I asked him to tell me the directions. Except I was too hungover to remember them, and it was starting to get very, very hot.

That's when I realized we need a CTU of one-night stands— a command center, just like in the show *24*, that is dedicated to getting you get laid . . . and then getting you out. Leave your favorite shirt in a girl's apartment but don't remember her name? CTU will send a SWAT team to recover it. Bang a busted chick who's gonna tell everyone? CTU will make her family disappear. Hook up with a girl in the middle of nowhere and leave at the crack of dawn? CTU will send a van to pick you up, and bring a bacon, egg, and cheese! The motto could be: "Helping you avoid the consequences of your actions since 2009."

GLOSSARY

DRIVE OF SHAME

A variation on the walk of shame in which you have to awkwardly drive the other person home in the morning. Only in LA will you ever wake up next to a girl in your own apartment, as I once did, and have her ask you to drive her home to Laguna Beach, a fucking two-hour drive . . . each way . . . or, in total, roughly four times as long as we spent actually hooking up.

Have you ever gone out, gotten bombed, gone home with someone, and then woken up so late the next day that when people saw you doing the walk of shame, they probably just assumed you were going out for the night . . . again? I don't think that's shameful; it's actually impressive. Especially now that I can see. A few years ago, I tossed my contact lenses for good and got LASIK eye surgery, which literally put my walks of shame in a whole new perspective. And after the Tucson incident, I got my first BlackBerry, then downloaded a GPS-enabled Google Maps application. I've never been more prepared to go into battle.

READY AND WILLING

Single guys feel the need to go out partying so much because if there's a chance that some girl, somewhere, is considering giving someone head, we want to make sure we're there to possibly receive it. Consistent action is not guaranteed, however. You know a buddy is on a pretty bad cold streak when he says to you, "Hey, you know that girl I hooked up with on that business trip last year? Yeah, I'm thinking about flying her in." It's never a good sign when you've given up on the millions of women in your own city and resorted to importing ass.

Unfortunately, whether it's due to missteps, poor timing, or just plain bad luck, every guy hits the occasional drought. In fact, regular Joes are just like professional athletes in that we both sometimes suffer inexplicable slumps. Whether it's tinkering with our technique or trying to grow facial hair, nothing seems to work. Our only solace is the knowledge that one night, when we least expect it, we'll hit a home run and get right back on track. But that doesn't make striking out any less painful.

Most women assume that guys think about sex all the time, and while I haven't done much to dispel those rumors, it's actually not true. We do not think about sex all the time. It's just that the slightest, most random erotic input takes us from not thinking about sex to needing to get off immediately, in 3.6 seconds. My penis is like the DVD player in your entertainment center—always in standby mode. If I turn on my computer in the middle of the afternoon and catch a glimpse of cleavage on a dating web site banner ad, well, that's a mandatory eight- to twelve-minute break right there. Followed by nap time.

I'm actually surprised at how vivid my imagination is sometimes. For example, my buddy Brandon used to claim he worked with the hottest girl ever. All we ever talked about was how hot his co-worker was. Now I have never met this woman, I have never even seen a picture of her, but I have pleasured myself to the thought of her about fifty times. I've created such an elaborate scenario in my head of banging this chick in Brandon's office—which I've never even been to, by the way—that I think if I ever do actually meet her, I might be disappointed. But the thing is, when I fantasize about having sex with this girl, she always turns to me and whispers, "Karo, you swear you won't tell Brandon about this?" And even in the dream I call up Brandon right away and say, "Dude, I just fucked the shit out of her!"

CHAPTER 4

PARTNERS IN PRIME

A true friend stabs you in the front.
OSCAR WILDE

It has been said that a friend is someone who knows all your flaws—and is still your friend. In my experience, a friend is someone who knows all your flaws—and seizes every single opportunity to make fun of you for them. As more of my buddies get hitched, they become much easier targets to rip on, but leave me with fewer bachelors to raise hell with. Being surrounded by like-minded dudes is one of the things that keeps a single guy sane—even if their presence is virtual. Sometimes I go months without seeing my best friends, but email and the occasional bachelor party are all that is needed to sustain male friendship for decades. On the other hand, if chicks don't see their friends for five days, they often cry and send each other texts complaining that they feel "distant." As I approached thirty and the prime of my life, my relationships with my boys evolved. Some fell by the wayside, while the tried-and-true ones became even closer. Married friends soon outnumbered single ones. But when all is said and done, my friends remain my gatekeepers—the filter through which I meet girls, make questionable decisions, and view the world. From wingmen to groomsmen, my buddies never cease to make life more entertaining—even if they prefer to laugh at me, not with me.

MAN'S BEST FRIENDS

Before my ten-year high school reunion in 2007, a lot of people told me that the best part of the event would be catching up with friends I'd lost touch with. But the weird thing was that I hadn't lost touch with any of my high school friends—not a single one. The guys I took a limo to the prom with were the exact same guys who decided to book a limo to take us out after the reunion. And we didn't get our security deposit back either time.

As I get older, it becomes a lot more difficult to keep track of where my friendships originated. But when I sit down and really think about it, my boys predominantly come from one of four segments of my life: high school, college, Wall Street, and Los Angeles. There's plenty of crossover, of course. For instance, two of my high school buddies were also in my fraternity at Penn. And two of my college buddies now live here in LA. Sometimes even I get confused. When I received some information about the upcoming reunion, I forwarded it on to my friend Chi, completely forgetting I hadn't even met him until four years *after* high school.

ADVICE

If you have a bunch of buddies over to drink in your apartment, never leave any personal effects lying around. At my last pre-game, my buddies found a to-do list of mine in the kitchen. The next morning, I noticed that after "fix window lock" they had added "buy K-Y Jelly and double-headed dildo."

The problem, in this age of Facebook, is that people are way too liberal with their use of the word "friend." A friend is not someone you've "tagged" in a photo. A friend is not someone you include on all your Evites and who includes you on all his Evites, even though neither of you ever responds. A friend is someone you can call and, if he doesn't call you right back, feel comfortable calling again and telling him he's a douche. A good friend is someone you call after a death in his family and he actually picks up, thus forcing you to awkwardly offer your condolences instead of leaving a voicemail like everyone else. A best friend is someone you've known for more than a decade, but if you had never met him before, and then hung out with him today for the very first time, you'd remark, "Wow. What a dick."

I've grown to appreciate my true friends more, especially since a lot of them are now on the complete opposite side of the country from me. I've quickly learned that no matter what I do when I visit New York, my East Coast friends will accuse me of being "*so* LA." Perhaps they're right though; maybe I have changed since moving west. In a way, I should be thankful they continue to call me out on it. Because one cannot experience bachelorhood full throttle without partners in prime. All of my friends keep me grounded by perpetually reminding me of every embarrassing moment in my entire life. My single friends keep me motivated by turning each night out into a competitive hunt for pussy. And my married friends keep me from second-guessing my decisions by demonstrating how the other half lives (within their means and without waking up on bathroom floors). At the end of the day, everyone serves a purpose—whether they like it or not.

CLAUDIO

Claudio is my oldest childhood guy friend. He's Argentine, and I believe that laid-back South American DNA has prevented him from ever being on time for anything in his entire life. I'm a very punctual person, and after knowing Claud for over twenty years, I still can't comprehend why he is always so late. He's like a fucking chick but instead of applying makeup and doing his hair, he just sits on the couch playing Madden until twenty minutes after we're supposed to meet at the bar.

Claud once told me that he and his roommate share the same bar of soap in their shower because it's cost-effective and soap is inherently clean. I argued that it's still disgusting, plus they're using the same total amount of soap, so that doesn't save money anyway. Eventually we agreed to disagree, though we all know the real winner is the one of us not sharing a bar of Irish Spring with his roommate.

THE WORLD OF CLAUDIO

Claudio once dated a chick with a very strange policy. She would only meet him in the middle. If they were going out to dinner, she was only willing to go to a restaurant equidistant from their apartments. If they were both out at different bars and wanted to meet up, she'd only go to a third-party bar in between. The last time they hooked up, I asked Claud how far he'd gotten. He said, "Halfway."

Claud has a soft spot for downing a few too many Captain and Cokes. One night, I was out with him and a girl he had been seeing for a few weeks. Claudio was absolutely hammered, and he accidentally referred to her as his girlfriend—right in front of her. When I mentioned it to him the next day, Claud didn't even remember the slip-up. The girl never said anything about it, so he just never brought it up. And that's pretty much how Claudio tackles dating dilemmas head-on.

Only guys thank their friends for *not* caring about them. After I had moved away, I got a frantic call from my buddies in New York asking if I'd spoken to Claudio. Apparently, they'd all gone out and gotten shitfaced, but no one had heard from Claud the entire next day. I dropped him a text but was generally unconcerned and soon forgot about it. Two days later, he resurfaced and explained that he was just really hungover and had lost his cell phone. I told him I figured as much but that everyone else was freaking out. Claudio replied fondly, "Karo, I knew you wouldn't be worried." "Hey," I said, "that's not what friends are for."

CHI

I met Chi (pronounced *chee*) when I was assigned the cubicle adjacent to his when I worked on Wall Street, before becoming a comedian. Chi and I became fast friends for two reasons. One, we shared a common interest in getting blindingly drunk after work. And two, I admired how he could get away with sporting a goatee and Diesel sneakers to the office (both against company policy) simply because he's Korean and people were afraid to say anything.

Everyone who meets Chi *loves* him. Compared to me, he's just a generally nice and friendly person. One time, he asked me to lend him some money and I obliged. Later, I was talking to another friend, and when the transaction with Chi came up, she remarked, "Chi's such a good guy." I was like, "Wait a minute, I'm the one who fucking lent *him* the money!"

People should really be fawning over me, and not Chi, after all I've done for the guy. First of all, I introduced him to his girlfriend, Cat. Sorta. What happened was, I was heading down to visit Penn in 2003 and invited Claudio and Chi to come party with me. Claudio brought his co-worker Cat, she and Chi hit it off on the car ride down, and they now live together. So basically I should be godfather to their future half-

Korean babies. Second of all, when I first met Chi, how can I put this ... the kid didn't wear underwear. Mind you, he didn't grow up in the backwoods of Seoul. He's from the fucking suburbs of Los Angeles, not far from where I live now. He just preferred to freeball until I sat him down one day and told him that's not how we do it in the real world. Put it this way—if you and I are co-workers, and *I'm* telling *you* to act more appropriately, something is seriously wrong.

THE WORLD OF CHI

No matter what the context, if I ever mention a female in conversation, Chi will always stop me and ask, "Wait, was she hot?" I'll say, "So the girl sitting next to me on the bus today was—" and Chi's like, "Whoa, hold on. She cute?" And if I tell him she wasn't, he gets a sad little look on his face and stops paying attention. I believe he has a mild form of ADD triggered only by the thought of unattractive women.

You may remember Chi from *Ruminations on Twenty-something Life* as my friend who once passed out drunk in the middle of a phone call and used all his minutes for the month in one night. I'm happy to report that he is much more tech-savvy now. He even locks his new BlackBerry with a password so that no one can use it if he loses it. Which is a great idea, except for the time he got so fucked up that he couldn't remember his own password and proceeded to enter it incorrectly ten consecutive times—which automatically triggers the BlackBerry to erase all the data in its memory.

But perhaps Chi's biggest flaw is that he makes the absolute worst plans ever. Back in the day, he organized a trip to visit his brother Danny at the University of Arizona. We took a red-eye from New York after work and got in very late Friday night, then flew out at like 5 a.m. on Sunday. Our entire stay was just over twenty-four hours. Quite frankly, I'm amazed we accomplished that much. Because Chi is also that guy who always misses his flight. We were both getting fucked up at this party once and I asked him, "Wait, aren't you going to Chicago tomorrow for work?" And he said, "Yeah, my flight is at 7 a.m., so I'm only gonna have a few more drinks." Then he calls me the next day like, "Dude, I'm still in the city. I overslept and missed my flight." And this happens *every time* he flies.

THE TRIPLETS

The Triplets are fraternal triplet brothers I went to high school with. I always refer to them by their birth order: Triplet #1 (the oldest, by two minutes) is a married risk manager, Triplet #2 is single and works in finance, and Triplet #3 (the youngest) is a married orthopedic surgeon. The Triplets are a good example of crossover friends, because I went to high school with all of them and college with two of them. Triplet #2 and I started at Penn together, and Triplet #3 later transferred there. I'll never forget when Trip 3 joined our frat as a sophomore yet already knew about all the hazing that was going to happen. I yelled at Trip 2, "Dude, why the hell did you tell him all the secrets about the House?" And he replied, "Karo, what were the odds that twelve months later my triplet brother was going to apply here, get accepted, transfer, rush, and pledge the exact same fraternity?"

Remember the classic *Seinfeld* episode where Jerry complains that the car rental place knows how to take reservations but not how to hold them? That's like Triplet #1 with plans: he can make plans; he just doesn't keep them. If you make plans with him, he tends to sort of pencil it in until something better comes along, and then cancels on you at the last possible moment. I love the kid, but sometimes we have to remind him that guy code clearly stipulates plans can only be broken for three reasons: a death in the family, the opportunity for sex, or playoff tickets.

THE WORLD OF THE TRIPLETS

I'm convinced the Triplets don't even make up a full human if you combine them. When I was still living in New York, I called Triplet #2 and made plans to go out that night. He said he didn't know what his brothers were doing. Later, Triplet #1 called me to see what I was up to. He also said he didn't know what his brothers were doing. Then I realized something—the three of them were in their apartment sitting within ten feet of each other the whole time.

Everyone's got the figure-out-the-check guy in their group of friends. As soon as the bill comes after a big dinner, I immediately pass it to Triplet #2. It is his sacred responsibility to divide up the bill among a dozen drunken idiots. And without fail, after all the money is counted, figure-out-the-check guy has to yell out, "OK, who didn't pay? Hello? Yo! Guys! Who the fuck didn't pay!?"

Once dinner is paid for, Trip 2 and I often end up boozing together, since his brothers are married and therefore dead to us. The bar is where Trip 2 takes on his alternate persona: the Hulk. Yup, besides figure-out-the-check guy, he's also the guy who gets drunk, gets into a fight, and ruins the night for everyone. Do not look at Trip 2 the wrong way or brush past him in a manner that could be construed as aggressive. He will punch you. You, in turn, will accidentally punch *me* in the face, as I'm standing right next to him. This has actually happened. Twice.

SHERMDOG

Shermdog is my fraternity brother whose prodigious success with the ladies is legendary, dating back to the night he lost his virginity . . . in a threesome. I still remember when Shermdog told me he banged a chick on the roof of our fraternity house—which shocked me because I didn't even know there was a way to get on the roof in the first place.

Junior year, Shermdog suddenly began suffering from chronic vertigo. For weeks he struggled to find the cause, until finally he discovered that he only got dizzy when he was sober, and that imbibing alcohol made the symptoms go away. I like to believe that this remarkable self-diagnosis led Shermdog to become the successful orthopedic surgeon he is today. I also believe that I won't let him near me with a scalpel unless he's had a few Jägerbombs first.

THE WORLD OF SHERMDOG

Do you have that one friend who still doesn't understand how to use email? That's Shermdog. When I send an email to all of my friends about something important, I always have to add at the end: "Will someone please call Shermdog and tell him, because I know he won't get this." In fact, I'm convinced he's completely incapable of functioning outside the hospital. I emailed him a link once and he called me ten hours later to tell me he couldn't figure out how to click on it. I asked him what he'd been doing all day, and he replied, "Brain surgery."

After college, Shermdog continued doing what he does best. One time I was out to dinner with him in New York when these cute chicks sat down at the table next to us and ordered sushi. I made some lame-ass joke, which they totally ignored. Then I went to the bathroom. By the time I came back, Shermdog was actually sitting at their table and feeding one of the girls a spicy tuna roll. He literally had them eating out of the palm of his hand.

My world was shaken in 2006 when Shermdog got a serious girlfriend, Sylvia, whom he now lives with. Just like with Chi, I'm the one who introduced them and thus deserve all the credit. Well, sorta. At my annual birthday pub crawl that year, Shermdog came with me, and Syl came with a friend of Chi's. They hit it off, and voilà: Shermdog missed the two subsequent crawls in order to attend girlfriend-related excursions. You see? I try to do something nice for my friends, and I always end up getting fucked.

BRIAN

That brings us to Brian, my childhood friend, my roommate in Manhattan from 2001 to 2004, and the first of my guy friends to get married (I served as his Best Man in 2006). Brian is the frequent recipient of barbs in my books and column, but with good reason: he is one of my major sources of comedic inspiration. The man has three basic needs: steak, sleep, and sports. His daily goal is to consume as much of each as possible. If he accomplishes that simple task, he considers it a day well spent. The guy is not out to save the world.

Throughout the years, I have commented on Brian's many strange quirks. But perhaps the most confounding is his quasi–speech impairment. Keep in mind that Brian is an Ivy League graduate (if you count Cornell) and works in finance. Yet for some reason, he pluralizes words that shouldn't be pluralized. For instance, he'll say, "Knock on woods," or call his wife "Babes." Once we were watching an old episode of *Saturday*

Night Live and he referred to the comedian onscreen as "Colins Quinn." Where he gets that extra *s* from, I have no idea. Brian also has a tendency to fumble over common phrases. He'll say, "I hunked the horn" (honked), "They're very tight-knitched" (tight-knit), "I was thrown through a loop" (for a loop), "I wrote it on a Post-Em" (Post-It), or even "She gave me the fifth degree" (third degree). And when I correct him, he'll say, "Odviously that's what I meant." And I'll say, "Brian, I love you to death, but the word is '*ob*viously.'"

THE WORLD OF BRIAN

Brian insists he would go to sleep at 7 p.m. if it were socially acceptable. He truly believes his life will only be moderately successful at best because he requires at least ten hours of sleep a night. He thinks it should qualify him for disability.

One might describe Brian and me as being like an old married couple, except instead of finishing each other's sentences, we finish each other's arguments. I'll ask him a question, but before he even opens his mouth, I'm able to recite his likely sarcastic response, followed by how he'll make fun of me for asking that question in the first place. I then start making fun of him for making fun of me. All before he's said a word. It's easier to just eliminate the middleman.

The last time Brian was job hunting, he asked me to give him a hand. Not wanting to pass up the opportunity to mock him—a newly minted MBA—for asking a comedian for help, I happily obliged and took a look at his résumé. My first piece of advice? Take out the "Hobbies" section. "Brian," I said, "you're married and almost thirty. Unless you've been building a soapbox derby racer that I don't know about, you don't have any *hobbies*."

Despite Brian living the life of a husband and me moving away to enjoy single life in LA, I still get a kick out of pretty much everything he does, especially when he employs his fondness for finance in seemingly pedestrian situations. When he was in LA recently, we went out for lunch. When I returned from a trip to the restroom, I found Brian studying the menu intently. Soon, he looked up and declared that if he ordered the regular Caesar salad and then added chicken, it would be five cents less expensive than if he just ordered the chicken Caesar. I was perplexed. Finally, he proclaimed proudly, "Don't you understand, Karo? I found an arbitrage opportunity in the appetizers!"

BRIAN AND BLAKE

When Brian and I moved in together after college, he was still dating his girlfriend from Cornell. When that relationship fell apart in a flaming wreck, we were both single for a while. Living in New York City with your best friend, both bachelors and making unnecessarily generous Wall Street salaries, well, that was the life. Alas, it was short-lived. One rainy night, at a bar on the East Side, Brian met a girl named

Blake (this one I can't take credit for). Nothing would ever be the same. I did my best to stop their impending relationship after they started hooking up. I told him not to call her. I told him not to see her. I was the typical single asshole roommate. But it was too late. Brian's parents came to the city for dinner one night and took him and Blake out instead of me. Not only was I losing my friend, but I was missing out on free meals as well. And that hurt more than anything.

While Brian and Blake have been married for three years now, and I love her very much, I was present for their relationship throughout its nascent stages. Very present. Because Blake spent most of her time in our tiny apartment. I once calculated that in one hundred-day period, Blake spent the night roughly ninety-five times, Brian stayed at her place three times, and twice they slept apart. One time, Brian and Blake went away for ten days on vacation. They came back after a really long flight and Blake came over directly from the airport and stayed for the next week. Don't you need a little break from each other? Don't you want to unpack? What the fuck is wrong with you people?

I explain all this because, in a way, Brian and Blake have had a major influence on my view of relationships. They had — and have — a great partnership. But, to me, it just seems so claustrophobic. I need my space and my independence. But most of all, I need to play the field. Twentysomethings were not meant to spend their days and nights with the same person. Variety is the spice of life. Instead of Brian and I acting like an old married couple, Brian and Blake *became* an old married couple. You know how traumatizing that was for

me? I actually used to yell at Brian for keeping the toilet seat
. . . down!

One of the aspects of their relationship that was most uncomfortable for me—and the part that will always scar me for
life—was jockeying for couch position. If I'd come home from
work and Brian and Blake were already on the couch, there
would really be nowhere for me to sit comfortably. Even
worse, they were always touching. Sometimes lightly caress-
ing, other times massaging, maybe even a little tickling, but
definitely always in contact with each other. Hello? Do you
see me? I'm here too! Have a little decency, for the love of God.
Sometimes I would try to plant myself in the middle of the
couch long before Brian and Blake got home, thus forcing
them to sit separately. It was like camping out all night for
concert tickets, though even more pathetic.

THE WORLD OF BRIAN AND BLAKE

When I lived with Brian—and, by extension, Blake as well—she would
make his lunch every day and they would go to bed by 10 p.m. at the
latest. Their one source of excitement? Watching reruns of *King of
Queens* with Kevin James. When I'd question him about it, Brian would
always say, "Karo, leave me alone. I live my life in syndication."

After Brian told me that he and Blake would soon be
moving in with each other, I began to wonder if, in his mind,
he was already married and living in the suburbs. One day, I

borrowed his keys and noticed that on his keychain were rows and rows of those little plastic bar code tags that you can swipe at the drugstore, the supermarket, Costco, etc. People are always telling me that I'm turning into my dad. But I never realized that Brian was turning into my mom.

Shortly after Brian and I parted ways and I moved into a studio a few blocks away, I had some friends over to booze and christen my new apartment. Everyone brought the requisite sixer. When Brian arrived with Blake, I noticed he was carrying a bottle of champagne. Immediately, I sensed something was amiss. Brian would never shell out for a bottle of bubbly just because I got a new place. Instinctively, I glanced over at Blake—and happened to spot a rock on her finger. And that's when I figured out that Brian had gotten engaged. Holy shit! A diamond ring? Dom Perignon? At age twenty-six? What happened to the Brian we all knew and loved? Then he whipped out some cheap plastic champagne glasses and I thought, "Oh, there he is."

As an engaged man, Brian's testicles quickly retracted. He once made the unfortunate mistake of traveling to Europe with a buddy and leaving an outgoing voicemail message that said: "I will be out of the country for two weeks. If you need immediate assistance, please contact my fiancée." Holy. Fucking. Shit. How could he leave a message like that? When Brian returned home he had about twenty-five voicemails from the boys requesting "assistance" from Blake for, among other sexual favors, "kissing my ass."

Though the beginning of their relationship left an indelible impression on me, I'm happy to report that Brian and

Blake are doing quite well. I've wondered, however, how Brian and I could know each other for so long, graduate from similar colleges, get similar jobs, move in together, and, eight years later, he could end up married and content and I could end up single and hungover. It gives new meaning to the nature versus nurture argument. Apparently, Brian was predisposed to marriage, because if he were influenced in any way by the environment I created in our apartment, he would still be my wingman. Instead, he's thinking about having kids and I'm thinking I could use another beer.

HOME AND VISITORS

My buddies in New York make a concerted effort to visit me here in LA. Customarily, when I crash at a buddy's place for more than just a night or two, I either take him out for a nice meal or buy him a bottle of vodka as a gesture of thanks. Last time Brian and Triplet #1 came out to LA, when the check came for our final breakfast, they announced they'd be picking up the tab to thank me for my hospitality. My share of the bill? Twelve dollars. Without compunction, I promptly began giving them shit for not having picked up a bigger check. Whoever said, "It's the thought that counts," probably never shamed his friends into buying him a handle of Goose.

I've noticed that when chicks have friends fly in to visit for the weekend, they don't go out that first night. They're like, "The girls are tired from flying. We're just gonna stay in and catch up." When my boys fly in for the weekend, they show up *wasted* and ready to go. I open the door when they get to my apartment, and they stumble in slurring, "We're not allowed on JetBlue anymore."

When girls visit each other, all the host has to do is organize one sixteen-girl dinner where everyone takes four hours to get ready and then just orders a salad. When my buddies are in town, it's like looking after little alcoholic baby chicks. I try to get them to all go in the same place, I have to feed them, clean up after them. When they finally decide to go to sleep at six in the morning, I make them a little bed of newspapers. My buddies don't really need anything to sleep on when they're crashing for the weekend—they're like Mac-Gyver. I'll say, "Sorry, bro, the couch is taken, and I don't have any extra pillows or blankets or sheets or anything." And my buddy will be like, "Don't worry about it, Karo. Just give me a mouse pad, a couple of garbage bags, and a wool hat. I will pass out!"

I've found that, when visiting my buddies, flying in on Thursday instead of Friday in order to get the long weekend in is never a good idea. Because every time I spend seventy-two hours drinking with friends I haven't seen in a while, by the final day, some shit goes down. The first night I get in, it's all, "What's up, dude, long time no see, let's get fucked up!" The second night it's Friday, it's the weekend, and my buddy is like, "I want you to meet some of my boys from work. Let's get fucked up!" The third night, a fight breaks out, someone gets arrested, chicks are crying, and I end up throwing up half in my friend's toilet and half on the side of his bathtub.

WINGMEN

A guy's primary responsibility to his friends is to act as a wingman. As I always say, "These chicks aren't gonna hit on themselves." An interesting dynamic I've noticed among my guy friends is how we take on different roles depending on whom we're with. For instance, although I'm quite gregarious and usually have no problem approaching girls, if I'm with Shermdog, I defer to him. He's even more adept and I've never seen him get shot down. But if I'm out with Triplet #2, who rarely speaks to strangers (unless he's in Hulk mode pummeling them into the ground), I'll be more assertive. The only time there's an issue is if two guys of equal strength are hanging out together. Then we end up approaching groups of women simultaneously and speaking over each other. We come off as aggressive and unorganized. Chicks can sense that bush-league shit a mile away.

There are times, though, when two guy friends are operating in perfect harmony, wingmanning each other into conversation after conversation with attractive women. If you spot two guys, one in front of the other, taking casual sips from their beers and slowly walking clockwise around the bar, they're doing what's known as "making a lap." Essentially we're flying in formation with the wingman in lead position. Results from this technique can be inconsistent, however. It's a great feeling when a buddy and I go out boozing, pick up two girls, and head to another bar with them. The only downside is when I get stuck sitting shotgun in the cab and have to awkwardly kick game to a girl in the backseat through the money slot in the partition.

NONVERBAL COMMUNICATION

When my buddies and I are prowling for chicks, we utilize a series of intricate hand signals and facial expressions to silently communicate with each other. If you observe closely at a really loud bar, you'll probably see guy code being employed across impressively large distances. Here are some of the common variations.

GESTURE	TRANSLATION
Subtle head nod	Self-admiration: "Dude, we're the coolest guys in here right now."
Raising beer in the air	Request: "Get me another one, and put it on *your* tab this time, asshole."
Mock gunshot to the head	Dismay: "The girl I'm talking to has a boyfriend" or "The girl I'm talking to is an investment banker."
Mimic holding two large melons	Approval: "Bro, the girl you're talking to has Civil War cannons!"
Smacking fist into palm of hand	Exhortation: "You gotta tap that. Otherwise I will."
Waving arms back and forth while mouthing the word "no!" (Also known as the "third base coach.")	Warning: "That chick is busted. Abort mission immediately; you're way too fucked up!"

While I always have my boys' backs, it's awkward when I'm at the bar and one of my buddies is hitting on a chick, but he's so sloppy drunk that I actually feel bad for the girl. No one likes to give his own friend the hook. But sometimes you gotta do it. And it's like dealing with a two-year-old. I have to approach my buddy delicately and say, "Hey man, it's time to go. Come on, let's clean that drool off you. No, let go of the nice girl's hand. Let go of her dress. No, she doesn't want your number, dude. Don't give her your cell phone. You're not helping. Look at her finger, bro. Will you look at her finger? You see that? Yeah, that's a wedding band. You got no shot, dude. What are you saying? Fine, I agree that married people should not be allowed in bars. That's a fair point. But we can't—no, we definitely can't kill her."

The frustrating part about wingmen is that they can turn on you so quickly. For instance, if a buddy introduces me to a chick in a bar, and I take her home and fuck her, it's congratulations all around. But if I dare admit that I have any feelings for her other than as a one-night stand, I get ripped apart unmercifully. I'll say to a buddy, "Hey, you remember that girl I hooked up with last week? She's actually pretty cool. I was thinking about maybe giving her a call and seeing if she wanted to go to the park or something." And my buddy will mockingly respond, "Oh, so you love her?" I'm like, "What are you talking about?" And he explains, "Well, if you're gonna take her to the fucking park, *obviously* you love her. You don't take someone to the park unless you're in love, Karo. But it's cute that you love her. Just admit that you love her. Admit that you love her right now in front of everyone!" And I'm like, "No, fine, I won't call her. I hate her. She's stupid!"

INSIGNIFICANT OTHERS

Every girlfriend I've ever had has said to me, "Karo, you're my best friend." And you know what? It's true. I *am* her best friend. Because when girls have a boyfriend, they rearrange their lives way more than guys do. You ever notice that when two close guy friends both have girlfriends, those girls always end up hanging out together? But the opposite is never true. When two girls who are friends both have boyfriends, those dudes don't spend time with each other unless absolutely necessary. That's because we still talk to our same twenty friends from high school and college every single day. You'll never hear a guy say to his girlfriend, "Baby, you're *my* best friend." Because it's just not true. Guys value longevity. You may be a great girlfriend, but in the scheme of things, you just got here. There's a pretty good chance I'm gonna do something dumb soon, and you're gonna break up with me. I don't run that risk with my boys.

When my frat buddy Jason moved in with his girlfriend (now wife), I always felt so awkward and immature when I called their home number and had to leave a message. It usually went something like this: "Hey Jason, it's Karo . . . uh, and, um, hi to you too, Jocelyn. Hello to the both of you, um, together. Uh oh, am I calling too late? Oh man, I'm definitely calling too late. You guys are probably sleeping. Or having sex. Oh God I shouldn't have said that. OK, uh, Jason, just give me a call back. Or Jocelyn, you can call me back too, I guess. I mean, I was calling for Jason but, you know, I don't want you to be insulted or anything. You know what? Maybe it's best if we never speak again."

Another frat buddy, Adam, lets his wife, Beth, access his email account and send replies pretending to be him because he's too lazy to write back himself. The best part is that she even tries to replicate his horrible grammar and spelling—though she hasn't quite perfected his unique syntax yet. So if I get an email from "Adam" that's properly capitalized or contains words with more than two syllables, I'm pretty sure it's an imposter.

OBSERVATION

Ever notice that the friends who only call you when their significant other is out of town are the ones who get the most upset when you can't hang out? My buddy Neil will call me and say, "Karo, what's up, dude? Let's go out and get fucked up tonight!" I'm like, "Bro, I'd love to, but I already have plans." He exclaims, "Don't be a fucking pussy, Karo. Just break your plans and come hang out with your boy!" I'm like, "Dude, I haven't heard from you in three months. What, is your girlfriend out of town?" There's a brief pause, and then he says, "Yeah, but that's not why I'm calling you." So I say, "OK, then let's hang out tomorrow night." He replies, "Uh, I can't." Me: "Girlfriend gonna be back in town?" Him: "Yeah . . ." Me: "Well, I hope she brings your balls back." Click.

I have a few platonic female friends who, before hanging up the phone, always say to me, "I love you." This usage is fine with me; after all, I do love them as friends. Take my college buddy Jen, for instance. The only problem is when she calls when I'm with a girl that I've been seeing, but haven't dropped the L-bomb on yet. We'll be lying in bed and my phone will ring. I pick up and the girl only hears my end of the conversation with Jen: "Hey, what's up? Yeah, uh huh. Listen, let me call you later. OK. Um, yeah . . . I love you too." And I can just see that look on the girl's face that says, "How much longer do I have to put up with shit before *I* get one of those?" My biggest fear is that a girl I'm dating is gonna come over to my apartment one day while I'm in the middle of something, and I'll say, "I love you." And she'll be like, "Oh my God, I love you too!" And I'll point to my ear and say, "Actually, I'm on my Bluetooth with Jen. Sorry?"

I think the relationship that guys have with their best friends can be summed up by the day in 2001 when Claudio's girlfriend dumped him. It was the same day that Brian and I, both single at the time, had finally secured entry to an exclusive Manhattan nightclub we'd been dying to hit up. That night, as Brian and I pre-gamed in our apartment, Claudio, obviously upset, called Brian. The phone rang and rang. I looked at Brian, but he didn't say anything or pick up. Finally, I understood—we couldn't get into the club with another dude, so Claudio, distraught or not, had to be sacrificed. We didn't tell Claud what happened until six years later, at which time he merely shrugged it off with a laugh in typical Claudio fashion. He accepted our explanation that we couldn't give up a night of possibly getting laid just to console him. That's not what friends are for.

His pugilistic tendencies notwithstanding, I've traveled with Triplet #2 to London, Sydney, and Buenos Aires. He's a great person to travel with because we have similar sightseeing protocols: skim the major landmarks and then hit the fucking bars hard. What is it about girls that makes them want to linger at every single plaque, rock, or tree? Guys are much more efficient. While swimming in Lake McKenzie, a top tourist spot in Australia featuring crystal-clear freshwater surrounded by white beaches and lush green forest, Trip 2 said to me, "Wow, this is beautiful." "Yeah, it really is," I replied. We both admired the landscape for a moment and then Trip 2 said, "I could leave in fifteen minutes," and I was like, "Totally."

I always like to have the most up-to-date information when I travel, so I splurged for a brand-new Fodor's Japan guide when I went to Tokyo with my Wall Street buddy Rob. The ever-miserly Rob, however, toted around an old, dog-eared Lonely Planet. I have to admit, though, occasionally he put me in my place. At one point, as he was trying to navigate, I said, "Dude, you have no idea what you're talking about; that guidebook is four years old!" "Karo," he replied calmly, "I'm not too worried. This temple was built in 738 A.D."

You know what I really hate about couples? That how long they've been in a relationship is directly proportional to how far in advance they make plans. You ever try to make plans with one of your married friends? I'll say, "Hey dude, wanna come over and watch the game?" He replies, "I can't, but how about six weeks from Tuesday?" My parents have a calendar in their kitchen that's booked until 2012. What are they doing, training for the Olympics? Plus, couples never make interesting plans. If I make plans eight months in advance, it's because I'm going to Barbados. If my married friends make plans eight months in advance, it's because they're going to brunch.

ADVICE

If you go out of your way to organize something fun for your buddies—a party, a dinner, or especially a vacation—you will end up getting the shaft. Someone won't pay, or will break something, or will otherwise embarrass you. This is the collateral damage that comes with trying to make plans for borderline alcoholics. Figure it into your costs ahead of time.

Bachelors and guys in relationships should also never go away on vacation together. Our objectives are completely different. If you're in a relationship and you go to an exotic country—even if you're not with your significant other—you want to explore, immerse yourself in the culture, eat interesting food, and walk along the water. When I go to a foreign country, I want to spend seven minutes at each of the five most famous sights, take three pictures, and then go find strange pussy.

The easiest way to tell if a guy is in a relationship is if the Facebook album from his trip contains a photograph shot while lying on a beach chair, looking past his feet and out onto the crystal blue water. What the fuck is that? I don't want to see your feet! Single dudes never take pictures like that. If I go on vacation, I will only show you pictures of some chick's tits, some dude vomiting, or a donkey. If I'm lucky, all three in one shot.

I've traveled around the world, but please don't ask me to do anything that involves roughing it. A few of my buddies went camping once and asked me if I wanted to come along. I asked them if there's a word more negative than "no." Since I moved to LA, my friend Scott has been trying to get me to go hiking with him. I always tell him, "Hiking really isn't my thing." And he's like, "How do you know if you've never even tried it?" I say, "Dude, I've been outside before. I get the gist."

BUSINESS CASUAL

Nothing brings the boys together like a never-ending game of reply-to-all. I don't know what it is about guys, being bored at work, and email that brings out the worst in all of us. It usually starts innocently enough. Once I sent an email to the crew asking for a bar recommendation. The first response came from Triplet #1, who—and I'm quoting verbatim here— suggested "Club Loser on 32nd and Nothington." That was followed by an email from Chi who recommended the ever-popular "Bar Blow Me on 69th and Your Mom Avenue." And those were the least offensive suggestions. The conversation soon degraded into name-calling until someone inevitably dropped an F-bomb, everyone using their work accounts feigned outrage, and then appended their Gmail addresses to the chain so that they could follow the discussion uncensored on their BlackBerrys. Just another day at the office.

One of my boys is staunchly opposed to me emailing anything remotely risqué to his work account, and I respect that. However, he just got rid of his personal cell phone because he got one through work, and now he doesn't want me texting him anything dirty either. I'm hamstrung. He says, "Karo, just don't curse." I say, "I'd rather not be friends."

The fact is, if you're emailing a bunch of buddies and find yourself adding, "PS: don't forward this on," you probably shouldn't be sending it in the first place. My all-time favorite, however, is the one guy in everyone's group who has an automatic signature in his work email that always seems totally out of place. He'll email me: "Yo Karo! Let's get fucked up tonight and score some sluts!" and at the bottom it will be signed: "Warm regards, Jonathan."

GLOSSARY

BROGREEMENT

I was at a house party in Santa Monica recently when my friend Jesse told me that he was leaving his job to work for his buddy on a film project. I congratulated him on the great news and for signing what must have been a lucrative offer. But Jesse replied that there was no formal contract, saying, "My buddy was just like, 'Bro, do you want to work on this?' And I was like, 'Dude, totally.'" And so a new term was born: the "brogreement"—a handshake transaction entered into by two close guy friends where no lawyers are involved (despite probably being necessary).

As we move up the ranks of our respective industries, I often find myself engaging with my friends in serious business. While this kind of networking is not surprising, it does take some compartmentalization. For instance, I was working on booking a venue for a stand-up tour with my buddy Brian (a different Brian) who is both a tour promoter in LA and a raging alcoholic. When we're talking contracts and financials on a Friday afternoon, he's a complete professional. But still, in the back of my mind, I'm thinking, "We better get this done soon, because in a few hours, this guy's gonna be obliterated."

My friends, of course, don't just use their business connections to help each other professionally, but also to help themselves socially. For instance, when women ask what he does for a living, my high school buddy Eric, who works in fixed income sales at a multinational investment bank, enjoys describing his job in the most unnecessarily complicated terms possible. I'm not sure if he thinks this will impress girls or merely confuse them into hooking up with him, but I have to admit that either way it works pretty well.

Then there are those of my friends who operate outside the realm of normal careers. As a comedian, I'm one of the few outliers. We also have my high school buddy Gadi. A happy-go-lucky Israeli, Gadi has a normal desk job by day—and works as a trance music DJ by night. In fact, he just played a huge trance festival in Acapulco. The show started at midnight and he went on last at 11 a.m., which I guess made him the headliner. The best part is that one of his early DJ stage names was E-Jekt. I guess only in the Israeli trance scene can you get away with calling yourself something that means "stop playing music."

FIRST OPINION

A lot of people hate doctors—they hate thinking about the doctor and they especially hate going to the doctor. Five of my best friends are doctors: surgeons Shermdog and Triplet #3, as well as Adam, Christina, and Seth, all of whom are anesthesiologists. Each of them fascinates me, probably because being a doctor is one of the few things I can't do. I mean, let's be honest, I *could* be a lawyer if I really wanted to. Law school would blow, but I could do it if I really tried. But I couldn't get past the first day of medical school without puking on a cadaver. That's why I love hearing about my doctor friends' jobs and lifestyles. I can't get enough. Even though when I go to their apartments to hang out they make me wait outside and read *Highlights* magazine.

Although traveling the country as a headlining comedian is thrilling, it will never hold a candle to being a doctor. When she was an intern, Christina called me up all excited and said, "Karo, you won't believe what happened today! This guy started seizing in the ER and I intubated him right there on the spot and I saved his life!" I was like, "Wow, Chris, that's amazing! Guess what? Today I wrote a joke about Chi freeballing!" It's just not quite the same rush.

> ## TERMINOLOGY
>
> Match Day is an annual event in March when fourth-year med students find out where they "match"—i.e., where in the country they will be spending the next three to seven years of their lives as residents. After matching, said med students go out and get demolished. In 2005, the year my friends went through the process, Match Day fell on both the first day of the NCAA tournament and St. Patrick's Day, making it a perfect alcoholic storm.

Sometimes, though, I feel a strange kinship with my doctor friends. I was talking to Shermdog once, and he was telling me that his cardiothoracic surgery rotation was starting in two hours. I was on the road at the time, and I told him I was getting ready for a huge show that started in two hours. He said, "I'm actually kind of nervous." And I was like, "Me too." Then he said, "Listen, I gotta go—I'm gonna jerk off." And I was like, "*Me too!*" Maybe I *could* be a doctor!

I remember sitting around with my buddies drinking beers after they took the MCAT, and they all said, "Some day, Karo, all this work will pay off and I'll treat you for free." Then most of them chickened out and became anesthesiologists, which is of no use to me. I did, however, recently have the misfortune of spraining my knee at the gym. A few weeks later, I saw Triplet #3 in New Orleans at his brother's bachelor party and asked him for an orthopedic consult. As he rolled up his sleeves, he asked me to fully relax my knee so that he could properly examine me. "Karo," he noted, "I wish all my patients were like you. You are remarkably relaxed." To which I replied, "Do you even realize how drunk I am right now?"

BOYS

There have been times in my life when I've looked around the bar to see Claudio, Chi, and Gadi, and felt like I was getting wasted at the United Nations. But despite our differences in appearance and nationality, those guys have always simply just been "my boys." Sure, women have "their girls," but there's a huge difference. Namely, your girls suck. Your girls change every season. Your girls are catty. One of your girls probably fucked your boyfriend. Female friendships are often contentious, jealousy-ridden, and, ultimately, ephemeral. But not so with my boys. Moving to Los Angeles was difficult, but whenever I get a text message from one of my boys back East telling me how big a shit he is currently taking, along with how little he misses me, I feel like I never left.

Dudes generally don't make new friends after about the age of twenty-five, so although I was lucky to have met a good group of guys in LA, I never quite knew where I stood. Until the night we sat around boozing in West Hollywood and Zach made fun of me, Justin laughed, and Neil high-fived Brian (the LA Brian). All at my expense. That's when I knew that I truly hated these guys—and that we were better friends than I thought.

The truth is, though, I was a little nervous when I left my friends behind in New York. I've always thought of myself as the connector, the nucleus of the group. Yes, the Triplets are brothers, but would they ever really hang out if I didn't make the plans? Luckily, I'm able to keep an eye on things at least once every November when my high school crew (plus Chi, of course) gathers at Peter Luger Steak House in Brooklyn for our annual holiday dinner. There we carry on a tradition of determining which one of us had the best year. For instance, the year that Brian got engaged and was accepted to business school, we declared it the "Year of the Brian." When Claudio got a new job, a new apartment, and a new girlfriend, we declared that the "Year of the Claudio." Sadly, there's never been a "Year of the Karo." That's not to say I've never had a great year; it's just that my accomplishments always seem to be too spread out. Plus, "new job" and "new girlfriend" aren't exactly categories I typically compete in. Maybe this will be my year. But if not, at least there will be something comforting about being at dinner surrounded by guys who wouldn't care if I went missing.

There is another type of brogreement implicit in all friendships: a solemn promise not to let your buddy become an asshole. Ever try to wear a shirt with lots of buttons or pockets, or get a radically new haircut? Your friends destroy you as soon as you enter the room. They're not doing it out of malice, but out of love. It's their job to make sure you stay true to yourself. As twisted as it seems, constantly denigrating each other's self-esteem ensures that no one ever gets too big a head—which is what so often leads to girls' friends being reduced to an ever-rotating panel of dyed blondes who don't share any history. For guys, this mechanism can mean giving you job advice or making you take off that fucking thumb ring before leaving the house. It is this solidarity that makes brogreements in the business world carry so much weight. After all, legal contracts can always be challenged in court, but who would dare renege on a commitment to a friend who once stopped you from popping your collar?

At thirty, the crux of male friendship is that our boys are now split into two camps—the single ones we carouse with and the married ones we only see on weekdays. But both groups are equally important. Bachelors need their friends in serious relationships. Whether it's someone to make fun of, a comfortable place to crash, or a glimpse at what middle age is like, my married buddies are a valuable resource. I solemnly swear to continue to give them shit, eat their food, and occasionally thank them for reminding me how much fun I'm having. The necessity of having single friends is just as crucial. They are not just wingmen, but also a means to better rationalize bachelorhood. My nocturnal adventures will always seem less deviant as long as I can point to a buddy I've known my entire adult life and say, "He was there too!"

CHAPTER 5

THE PURSUIT OF HAPPY HOUR

*I have taken more out of alcohol than alcohol
has taken out of me.*
WINSTON CHURCHILL

I think that people's reaction when I tell them that I don't drink coffee is equivalent to my reaction when people tell me that they don't drink alcohol. The fact is, getting drunk is an American tradition—one could say the values we cherish most include life, liberty, and the pursuit of happy hour. I was indoctrinated into the culture at an early age. The first time I ever got smashed—at the Triplets' house, in high school—is still the drunkest I've ever been. I threw up in a popcorn bowl for five hours straight and haven't touched a screwdriver since. But that hasn't stopped nightlife—with its allure of endless liquor and chicks whose principles are degraded by said liquor—from becoming an integral component of my bachelor experience. When presented with the prospect of hitting the bars after a long day, single dudes carefully consider their options. The angel on one shoulder says, "Stay home! You're gonna have four overpriced beers and get shot down by every girl anyway." The devil on the other shoulder says, "But if you go out, you might get laid. You don't want to pass up some ass, do you?" Ever wonder where the devil is later, when you're paying for those expensive drinks and there's not a chick in sight? I bet he's trying to bang the angel.

PICK YOUR POISON

It's a simple fact that once you get married, you go out and get drunk less frequently. Often this is simply because making plans for two downtrodden people is more difficult than making plans for one person who has no obligations or moral center. Another reason is that married guys really have no need to enter the meat markets I call bars. They've found their prize and are now content to have a glass of wine at dinner and cry themselves to sleep. For bachelors intent on landing their next one-night stand, though, there is no other option besides picking our poison and heading out on the town. We'll rest when we're forty.

I'm always dumbfounded when, in the movies, one guy asks another guy if he'd like a drink, then just pours into a glass with ice cubes some generic brown liquor, which the other guy proceeds to drink, no questions asked. At what age do all men receive a memo declaring that they must accept and enjoy any brown liquor handed to them? Because I certainly didn't get it. I stick to the classics: vodka and beer. If I was at a buddy's place and he asked me if I'd like a drink, and then he just started pouring scotch into my glass, I'd be like, "What the fuck are you doing? You got Amstel or something?"

I hate bars that have a selection of, like, five hundred different beers. If I wanted to feel like an idiot ordering from an overly extensive and confusing menu, I'd drink wine. I'm a man who likes his beer served in a red Solo cup with a hint of Ping-Pong ball residue. Keep it simple. (Side note: Apparently, attempting to cleanse Ping-Pong balls by repeatedly dipping them into the same cup of tepid water is not hygienic. Who knew?)

When I offer to buy a chick a drink and she asks for a martini, I know I'm in for a world of hurt. That is the most poorly designed glass I have ever encountered. When a girl requests a dirty, essentially what she's saying is that either I'm getting martini all over my sleeve, or she's getting it down her cleavage as I try to hand it to her.

OBSERVATION

Mixed drinks are like masturbation: only you know exactly how you like it.

When I switch to the hard stuff, I follow a few tried-and-true rules. During the afternoon, I never drink the soda or juice that I might be using later that night to mix with liquor.

Cocktails taste much better if you haven't recently tasted the mixers on their own. I also only drink mixed drinks that I make myself. I just don't like other people making my drinks and I hate the weak shit that bartenders mix. So once I get to the bar, I'm all about vodka on the rocks. And, finally, I try never to buy tequila shots unless I'm in Mexico. Very bad things happen when I drink tequila stateside. I mean, very bad things happen when I drink tequila in Mexico too, but at least I'm experiencing the local culture.

I'm always the guy who gets a stray ice chip in his shot. It's horrible because, for a millisecond, I think I'm gonna choke to death. Then I finally swallow, remember how much I despise SoCo lime shots, and wish the ice chip had just finished me off.

When I'm at the bar and I take that one extra, totally unnecessary shot, I end up having to give *myself* a pep talk. I rip the ill-advised shot and then start muttering under my breath, "Oh God, that was a bad idea. I'm starting to salivate . . . please don't puke. Choke it back. Choke it back, Karo! Try not to cry. Where's the bathroom? *No*, if you puke you're gonna have to start drinking all over again and you have such a great base going. Just breathe. Breathe . . . OK . . . I think it passed. OK, one more shot."

DUE DILIGENCE

When I'm going to a bar, I concern myself with only two questions: are there gonna be chicks there, and can I get in? If

I tell a girl about a bar, the first thing she asks is, "What kind of music do they play?" Honestly, if I think about the last ten bars I've been to, I couldn't name one song that was played. Bon Jovi could show up and do a surprise set and I'd be completely oblivious.

If I'm researching bars online before going out, I turn to Citysearch. But what always bothers me about the negative user reviews is that they're often written by someone who only went to the bar once, couldn't get in, and is really pissed off about it. You don't see a lot of truly candid positive user reviews. Probably because they'd sound something like this: "I never heard of this bar, but this chick I texted told me to meet her there. I was real fucked up so I don't really remember what the place looked like. I threw up in a urinal in the bathroom and I lost my credit card. The girl I texted ended up ditching me but I went home with some other girl whose name I did not know and she touched my penis. This bar rocks and I'd go back again if I could find it."

And if I'm having a birthday party or something, and I ask a girl to recommend a bar, she'll always ask, "Well, what are you looking for? Because this one place has a jukebox and they play fun '80s music and then at midnight there's a DJ and you can dance and it's *so* fun!" And I'm like, "Um, I'm looking for *not* that." If one of my buddies says, "I went to this bar once, I don't know if it was that good, but I met this chick there and I got a blow job—" I interrupt, "Done! That's where we're going! Sold to the place where my buddy once got a blow job!"

> ### *OBSERVATION*
>
> Have you ever been to a swanky club in the middle of the day when the lights were on and seen how disgusting it actually is?

Here's an experiment: pick a bar that you go to a lot, then ask a friend how many people he or she thinks it holds. They'll inevitably respond with, "I don't know. I'm not good with that kind of stuff." I've never heard one person ever claim basic competence at being able to gauge how many people can fit in a room. I bet even the fire marshals who post those annoying capacity signs are just making it up.

Despite the fact that Los Angeles is full of ridiculous, *Entourage*-worthy tail, I still believe that this city is severely lacking in nightlife. Sure there are cool bars, but there are fewer of them, they're much farther away from each other, and they're much harder to get into than any other city I've partied in. Plus, the weird thing is that all the venues are either shitty dives or really upscale—there's nothing in between. In LA, there is no Goldilocks of bars.

Every major city should have a designated district of karaoke bars, thus preventing me from walking into one by accident. Nothing is worse than enjoying a mellow evening of binge drinking with the boys when suddenly some chick starts belting out "Like a Virgin" from a karaoke machine at a volume fifty decibels louder than a space shuttle launch. In a perfect world, karaoke would be limited to bachelorette parties and Tokyo.

THE PRE-GAME

Most sloppy nights in the life of a bachelor are not spontaneous. When it comes to getting drunk, premeditation means knowing ahead of time that tonight you're gonna do something *dumb*. It's been a long week of work, you haven't been out in a while, the whole crew is finally together, and before that first round even comes, you're thinking to yourself, "In a few hours, I am planning on doing something I'll regret."

TERMINOLOGY

To me, the phrase "Let's grab a drink" is both the rallying cry and the secret password of bachelors everywhere. For some reason, no one uses that phrase until they've graduated college, and then they use it so frequently it becomes virtually devoid of meaning. If you really think about it, you only actually grab a drink with about 10 percent of the people you say it to. Of that 10 percent, most think you literally want to have a solitary cocktail and exchange pleasantries or discuss current events (these people are often married or lawyers). The remainder—whom you quickly recognize as kindred spirits—take "grab a drink" to mean "let's get black-out shithammered."

My buddies routinely call me up and say, "Karo, you have to come to this bar. There's a 25 percent chance there may be cute chicks there." And I say, "Dude, I have the flu, I have a funeral at eight o'clock in the morning, it's pouring outside ... I'll be there in twenty minutes." Girls call their friends and say, "Kate, you have to come to this party, there's definitely gonna be a ton of cute boys there. *And* it's open bar. *And* we'll pick you up." And she's like, "I don't know ... I'm wearing really comfy sweatpants." What is it about an elastic waistband that makes it such an obstacle for chicks to leave the house? I can just imagine the girl's roommate yelling, "Kate! We gotta go! The building's on fire! We have to evacuate!" And she's like, "But I'm wearing these sweatpants. I'm on the couch. *Grey's* is on ..."

I'm sorry, but wasted Saturday night plans must be confirmed. Ever run into a friend you haven't seen in a while at the bar on a Saturday night, and in between shots of Jäger and your twentieth beer, you make plans to get lunch or something the following week? And then your friend gets mad at you for standing him up when you don't show? I don't think that's fair. Standing someone up implies you knew you had plans and chose to ignore them. But having no recollection of meeting the person in the first place should absolve you of all wrongdoing.

WHERE'S THE BAR?

I recently went to a bar where the cross street was actually Cross Street. Trying to explain to my friends how to get there was like playing drunken "Who's on First?"

On the East Coast, you have to dress up to go out—everyone's been negged at one time or another for trying to wear sneakers into a club. On the West Coast, you have to dress down to go out. Really down. When I'm standing in front of the mirror in my apartment in LA on a Saturday night, I often think to myself, "Wow, I look way too nice right now. I match so well they might not even let me in. Hmm, I should muss up my hair, throw on some flip-flops, ripped jeans, a mesh hat, and a weird thrift-store tuxedo shirt. Yeah, then I'd fit in."

VELVET DOPES

I still enjoy going out as much as I used to, but I've long since given up on going to any lounge or club that might be hard to get into or involve waiting on line. I'm so over that shit. And please, don't insult my intelligence by even mentioning the word "list." Seriously, I'm thirty years old and I've been through this countless times. The list does not work. The list will not get you in. The list does not exist. Get the fuck out of my face. But, um, you know what . . . why don't you put me on it anyway. You know, just in case.

Still, every once in a while—in a moment of weakness—I'll agree to go out somewhere like that and soon find myself arguing with a chick wielding a clipboard. The weekend should be about unwinding with friends and drunkenly hitting on everything that moves—not about playing games with someone beneath me just so I can go inside and take a fucking piss.

When it comes to getting into an exclusive bar, guys suddenly lose all their ability to estimate. You know when you call inside the club and the dude who is going to help you get in asks who you're with? I quickly survey the eleven guys and one girl that is my crew and then say, "Um . . . it's like two or three dudes and, uh, like six girls, six or seven girls." Then I end up on the sidewalk trying frantically to recruit stray chicks to come in with us in order to counterbalance the aggressive amount of cock that I'm rolling with. The desperation makes me feel like a telemarketer. A girl walks by and I'm like, "Excuse me. Hi, how are you? Would you be interested in coming in—no, wait. No, come back. Shit!"

I often find that the bar next door to the more exclusive bar that I really wanted to get into but couldn't is more fun anyway. And that's not because I'm bitter or anything. The truth is, if I show up at a lounge with five dudes, and they laugh before barring us from entry, I fume with anger. But if we go somewhere else with the same ratio and get right in, I question why any decent establishment would allow such a thing.

OBSERVATION

The longer the line outside a bar, the worse it sucks to wait, but the better it feels when you walk past everyone on your way in.

When I go headlong into the night, there's always one foe who's determined to make me wish I stayed home: the bouncer.

My all-time favorite bouncerism is when the guy says he can't let anybody else into the bar because the fire marshal will shut the place down. I never imagine some bean-counter posting capacity signs, but rather a burly fireman with a giant hat, an axe, and a hose running up to the bar yelling, "We got a call that this place is full of dudes!"

Sometimes I wonder if bouncers have a certain quota of people they have to throw out of bars in a given month. Seriously, why isn't there a bouncer code of conduct? If you get treated unfairly, there's no recourse, save for writing a nasty review on Citysearch that just makes you sound like a petulant douche. Bouncers should be moved from bars to stadiums and airports, where they could eject inebriated fans of the opposing team and unceremoniously pound on idiots who still don't realize they have to take their shoes off before going through the fucking metal detector.

Just like certain restaurants have a BYOB policy that allows you to bring your own wine, clubs should let you bring your own bottles of liquor. You would still pay for beer and mixers, as well as a small corkage fee. Admittedly, this idea would never fly, but at the very least let's stop referring to paying five hundred dollars for a bottle of Absolut as bottle "service." It should more accurately be described as getting torn a new asshole but at least having a booth to sit down and rest it.

I just don't think I'll ever get used to going out in LA. On one hand, I respect the fact that there are some lounges here that are so exclusive they don't even *have* a line—either you get right in or you never get in. At least they're upfront and don't waste your time. On the other hand, just when I think

I've got LA nailed, she bitch-slaps me in the face. It's a Saturday night, I know exactly where I'm going, exactly what time to go, and exactly whom to ask for when I get there. Then I roll up in a cab only to see a red carpet, spotlights in the sky, and paparazzi everywhere because the club is closed for a movie premiere. Fuck me.

PUB LIFE

Some of my buddies used to play Erotic Photo Hunt, which is an electronic bar game that shows you two pictures of naked chicks and challenges you to find the differences. Then one day the local bar changed it from Erotic Photo Hunt to regular Photo Hunt. Suddenly we were counting how many petals were on the daisy a little girl was holding and it just became weird. However, the electronic novelty that all bars should be required to have is a photo booth. These amazing devices enable you to hook up with a chick in private, without having to leave the bar, plus you get the pictures as proof. Try doing that with Buck Hunter.

Do good architects consider themselves above designing bars? I can't think of any other structures that are laid out so poorly. Most seem to sport the "hourglass" shape in which the front of the bar connects to the back via a narrow channel barely big enough for a single red blood cell to pass through. Plus that's the way to the bathroom. Where there's one toilet for two hundred wasted people. And it's broken.

> ### *GLOSSARY*
>
> **REFILL LIMBO**
> Occurs when you're having casual drinks with friends, they order another round from the waitress, but you still have half of your beer remaining and are momentarily unable to decide whether to order and chug or pass and sip.

Let's take all of the bathroom attendants out of bars in LA, New York, and Miami and, like bouncers, put them in stadiums and airports where they're desperately needed. It's a waste to have attendants manning bathrooms in bars where their sole purpose is to provide obnoxious kids a cleaner surface to blow lines off of.

You've never seen a guy prouder of himself than when he's pissing in the bar bathroom with no hands. Every time I go in there, guys are unzipping at the urinal, putting their hands on their hips or behind their heads, and exulting in what they have accomplished. Other guys, however, get enraged when someone takes a shit in the bar bathroom. They stamp around yelling, "It fucking reeks! I'm gonna find the guy who did this!" You want to find the guy who took a dump in the bar bathroom, huh? I'll tell you who it is—it's the happiest guy here.

LADIES' NIGHT

Occasionally, I'll be hitting on a girl in a bar and just know I don't have a shot. Things will be going pretty well, and then I'll ask, "Can I get you a drink?" And she responds, "Actually, I don't drink." Sometimes she's just trying to get rid of me, but when she's actually being serious about not drinking, I'm devastated. I mean, how am I supposed to take a chick home if she's sober but I'm wasted? That's like trying to beat a team in football when they have your playbook. I just want to shake her hand and say, "Well, it was great meeting you, but clearly this isn't working out. I'm gonna go find someone whose decision-making abilities are a bit more impaired."

OBSERVATION

The only thing worse than talking to a girl at a bar and not realizing that you're wasted, slurring, and swaying, is talking to a girl at a bar and *knowing* that you're wasted, slurring, and swaying. My gut tells me to stay the course. But the look on her face tells me she's horrified.

I think there should be a law against UPT—ugly people touching. Have you ever noticed that the ugliest couple at the bar is always all over each other? And they both have all these weird pimples and rashes and shit? Listen, I know you're excited to have finally found the only human on earth actually willing to go down on you, but I'm gonna vomit in my fucking beer if you don't stop slobbering on each other.

If the situation at the bar is dire and I've gone through my list of usual booty texts, sometimes I'll drop a line to a one-night stand from like three years ago. If she never responds, I automatically assume she's engaged. But sometimes she responds right away to tell me she actually *is* engaged. The message is always something like: "yeah I was just tired of going to the same shitty bars and getting drunk every night like an idiot. so what's up w/ u?" And I sheepishly put my BlackBerry down and order another twenty-five-cent pitcher.

PUT IT ON MY TAB!

I was partying it up after a show in Chicago when I accomplished a first for me: I had two different tabs on two different cards open simultaneously at the same bar. Some might call this reckless. I call it "building credit history."

Whenever I end up at a campus bar while on tour, it's an opportunity to relive my glory days. I was once at a bar at Northwestern that was having a special that was something like $2.50 for a thirty-two-ounce beer—essentially, a shitload of beer for very little money. I ran up a $175 tab. Turns out that when I'm back at college, the cheaper the special, the more likely I am to buy rounds for everyone of everything *but* the special. So essentially the exact opposite of what I was like in college.

> ### *ETIQUETTE*
>
> If you're a male friend of mine and I offer to buy you a drink, order
> a beer. I was just being nice and didn't expect you to request a
> Long Island iced tea with four top-shelf liquors. Do I look like I'm
> trying to fuck you?

Even when I'm in a situation where I can't pay with a
credit card, I still manage to throw money away for no reason.
Once I drunkenly tossed a crumpled-up hundred-dollar bill
at a recalcitrant cab driver. Which would have been obnoxious enough had I not added, "Say hello to Benjamin McKenzie." I'm pretty sure I meant Benjamin Franklin—whose face
is on the bill—and not the actor who played Ryan on *The OC*.

PARTY LIKE A ROCK STAR

Two of the maxims that I try to live by are related: work
hard and play harder, and go hard or go home. In other words:
take care of your responsibilities before getting absolutely
destroyed; but if you're *not* gonna get absolutely destroyed,
don't even bother showing up at all. Let's face facts: I've been
out of college for eight years. But that doesn't mean I can't
still party like a rock star. I really look at myself as a twenty-
first-century Peter Pan: it's not, "I won't grow up"; it's more

like, "I will grow up—as long as I can still throw up every other weekend."

Whenever someone says to me, "I don't have to drink to have a good time," my response is always, "Well, I do." Have you ever been sick or the designated driver and gone out with your best friends in the whole world when they're drinking but you're not? It's not fun *at all*. Not even a little bit. I try to pretend like I'm having a great time but secretly I can't wait to get home, strip down to my boxers, and just watch the shit out of my DVR. I think that going out with your buddies when they're fucked up and you're not is actually detrimental to your friendship, because you realize what jackasses they are. I'm looking around thinking, "Good thing I'm not like that when *I'm* drunk."

GLOSSARY

BLOODBATH

An event of epic drunken debauchery. As in, "Dude, I hear this party tonight is open bar." "Really? It's gonna be a fucking bloodbath."

Ever say goodbye to everyone after a long night and then get halfway down the block only to realize you forgot your jacket? You always have to go back, acknowledge the weird looks everybody's giving you, respond to irritating little gibes like, "Hey! Back already?" then reclaim your jacket and hoist it skyward while doing a half-lap around to demonstrate to the gathering crowd that all is well and you've simply returned to retrieve the North Face you now rue ever having purchased.

As the hour grows later and later and my friends and I grow drunker and drunker, I become increasingly vigilant about which bar to head to next. As soon as it passes 1 a.m., I always start suggesting bars closer and closer to home. I'll say, "How about that lounge at Hollywood and Ivar? No? OK, what about that new place on Santa Monica and Fuller? No? OK, OK, how about that bar on Melrose and Harper? How about that, huh?" And my friends are like, "Karo, there's no bar there. That's your apartment."

VOLUNTARY ALCOHOLISM

I don't need to drink every day. But when I do drink, I have absolutely no self-control and get obliterated every single time. I either have zero drinks or fifty drinks. I call this condition "voluntary alcoholism." You know you're a voluntary alcoholic if . . .

➤ You've never tasted Red Bull without vodka in it.
➤ You go straight from work to the bar and stay until last call. Even though you always lose your laptop bag.
➤ You've known so far ahead of time how fucked up you're gonna get that you've called in sick for work the next day—before you even went out.
➤ When you're pre-gaming with your buddies, and you have to take a shit, you take your drink with you.

> ➤ When you get to a party and there are no cups left, you'll drink out of anything. That includes the children's Dimetapp dispenser you find in the cupboard. Example: "Yo dude, let me get to the keg! Come on, I've got two teaspoons here! I'm taking the twelve and older dose. Goddamn it. It's all foam!"

> ➤ When you get to a party two hours late and everyone's already wasted, you totally panic, overcompensate, start lapping people, and end up getting twice as fucked up as anyone else.

> ➤ When you go to the bar and order two beers, and your friend asks who the other one's for, your response is, "I don't understand the question."

TAKE IT TO THE HOUSE

No matter how old I get, there will always be a special place in my heart for good old-fashioned house parties. I'm not the only one. There's an entire faction of twentysomethings and thirtysomethings out there who live seemingly mature lives—but only to the naked eye. Take my friend Mike, an accomplished software developer in New York whose downtown apartment has actually been passed down for years to successive generations of graduates from his fraternity—like an off-campus party house. Or my buddy Justin, a producer here in LA who had trouble finding a new apartment because he couldn't find one big enough to fit his beer-pong table. Unfortunately for him, "Hardwood floor quickly soaks up cheap beer" is typically not an amenity found on Craigslist.

Women my age have stupid fucking birthday parties. I love that they wear a little party dress and tiara, crimp their hair, and invite five hundred dudes. That's if their party is at a bar; if they decide to have it at an apartment, it's even worse. You see, despite my penchant for taking over a friend's house for a rager, one thing I outgrew years ago is dressing up. On average, one in four Evites I receive from chicks is for some sort of elaborate costume/theme party that reminds me of sophomore year. If you're a strong, independent woman nearing thirty, you should not be throwing parties entitled Pimps & Hos, Forties & Hos, or Golf Pros & Tennis Hos. Unless you want to do Regular Guys & Hos, in which case I'm in.

The last time Justin (he of beer-pong table fame) had his annual Super Bowl party, he decided not to get a keg because it was just too much of a mess. That turned the first quarter festivities into a game of "Let's see how many fucking beers we can jam into this fridge." The thing is, given all our combined years of drinking experience, I am still struck by my friends' complete inability to purchase the right amount of booze. It's an inexact science by any measure. I feel like half the time the cups, ice, and liquor run out in about forty-five minutes, and the rest of the time the party's host is left with a bounty of alcohol so great that ten months later I find myself back at my buddy's place polishing off a frosted-over bottle of Skyy and asking, "Wait, dude, is this left over from St. Patrick's Day?"

GLOSSARY

CBP AND SECOND-ROUND EVITES

Sometimes I'll go weeks and months without a birthday party, and then all of a sudden I simultaneously receive a dozen different Evites from friends of various backgrounds inviting me to shindigs, blowouts, and the occasional bash, all to celebrate their birthdays . . . on the same night. CBP, or Clustered Birthday Phenomenon, occurs without any logical explanation. It is a dangerous epidemic too, usually resulting in exorbitant amounts of money being spent at annoying parties with people I don't really like.

And have you ever opened an Evite as soon as you received it, noticed that over a hundred people had already responded, and then realized that the host blatantly forgot to include you the first time? Receiving a Second-Round Evite usually makes me want to attend said party even less than I did before, which is damn near impossible.

If anything is going to stop an all-night rager from continuing, it's not gonna be the neighbors or the cops. It's gonna be that guy with the downstairs bathroom that gets all fucked up when you have a party. I always feel bad for downstairs bathroom guy as I'm pissing on his toilet seat and rifling through his year-old copies of *Maxim*. Strangely enough, though, the next morning I forget all about him.

Walk-up apartments on really high floors can be great for parties, because whenever someone gets to the door it's a grand entrance—newcomers exult in having made it all the way up and then comically overdo the heavy breathing. Plus, the party goes all night because people would rather drink stale beer and make idle conversation than climb back down all those fucking stairs.

Ultimately, my favorite thing about house parties is that they usually present a rare opportunity to do kegstands. I actually once cut my lip trying to do a kegstand. And when I say "once" I mean it was less than a year ago. That's right, I still enjoy the occasional kegstand. To me, a kegstand is the ultimate display of defiance. Because a kegstand requires two things that are not always readily available: a keg and enough crazy friends willing to hold you up. When you get to be my age and can still look around to find both, well, life is good.

WASTED

For the past six years, I've organized a mid-afternoon pub crawl through New York City for my friends in lieu of a birthday party. There's just something about drinking during the day that appeals to me. I think it might be the drinking during the day part. When I turned thirty, I decided that would be the last year. I don't know, for some reason vomiting in the street in broad daylight seems fine at twenty-nine but a little uncouth at thirty-one.

I wouldn't say I'm a bad drunk, just an inefficient one. I tend to lose all short-term memory. One night when I was still living in New York, Chi called me sixteen times to tell me where to meet him. By the time each call ended and I put the phone in my pocket, I had forgotten the address. Chi also likes to say that I'm a terrible person to tell your secrets to because I get drunk and reveal them. But technically that's not true. I usually get drunk and reveal my own secrets, which is actually worse.

It bothers me that every liquor ad has a little line at the bottom that says, "Enjoy responsibly." First of all, you can't really enjoy liquor responsibly—that's an oxymoron. Furthermore, responsibility is subjective. When Triplet #2 was living in London for a year, I visited him, drank too much, and threw up in his apartment. That was irresponsible. But I threw up in the garbage can, which was responsible. But the garbage can didn't have a bag in it, which was irresponsible. And it was mesh, which is just plain gross.

When I was with Triplet #2 in Australia, I took him out for his birthday. Our other friend on the trip, Jen, was able to get us upgraded to a gourmet suite in the Sydney Marriott. This worked out well, as I was able to utilize the bucket that held our complimentary champagne to vomit in profusely after taking three birthday shots for every one of Trip 2's. The following day, we were scheduled to climb the Sydney Harbour Bridge, the top of which offers spectacular views of the Opera House and the rest of the city. Unfortunately for me, one of the prerequisites for scaling the bridge was passing a breathalyzer test. Even at 3 p.m. the day *after* drinking, I still failed. Don't judge me.

GLOSSARY

DBD

Traditionally, I write the acronym DBD in black Sharpie on the back of my left hand before any drinking binge I predict will turn into a total bloodbath. These events typically include my birthday and New Year's Eve, as well as a few wild cards such as weddings and Yankees playoff games. DBD stands for Don't Be Dumb and is meant to remind me during moments of severe inebriation not to do or say anything stupid. Has almost never worked.

One year I was out boozing with the boys in South Beach when I started to get that tickle in the back of my throat. Of course, my first instinct was to throw up *in* my BlackBerry. I literally took my BlackBerry out of my pocket, held it in front of my mouth, unlocked it, and then vomited into the keyboard—into the nooks and the crannies. Broke it completely. But the worst part was calling T-Mobile and trying to get a new phone. I was sitting there in Miami with my fucking PukeBerry, talking to the customer service rep, and he wanted to start "troubleshooting." I remember the guy said, "When you go to Tools, then Options, what do you see?" I scrolled through, looked at the screen, and was like, "Um, pizza. And some corn." There's always corn in there, right? I don't even eat corn. Forget about fixing the phone, I just wanted to know where all that corn came from.

I once dated a girl who claimed to be a raging party animal like myself. However, no one gets drunk and embarrasses himself quite like I do. When this chick claimed to be a bigger idiot than me when wasted, I actually took offense. I said, "Are you saying that if we were equally drunk, you could out-embarrass me? No way!" And she was like, "But Karo, if I'm drunk and someone tells me to do something stupid, I'll do it." I said, "Darling, if I'm drunk, I come up with the stupid ideas myself *and* execute them. I'm like a one-stop shop of embarrassment." That really put her in her place.

When I hear a tale of drunken woe—a friend who pissed off his girlfriend so bad she broke up with him, or a chick falling down a flight of stairs—my first reaction isn't empathy, it's relief. "Thank God that wasn't me." I've just been on the business end of too many inebriated disasters. I've found that sometimes the most discomfort occurs not right after I make a faux pas, but later, when I try to apologize for it. Many years ago I was out with my buddy Zach and I just completely insulted his girlfriend right in front of him. I believe I told the girl I wanted to "fuck her sideways," which doesn't even really make sense. The worst part, however, was calling Zach a few days later to apologize—and waking him up. Saying "I'm sorry" to someone you just jolted out of a deep slumber merely adds injury to insult.

One of the side effects of voluntary alcoholism is amnesia. Nobody likes that call from a friend the morning after who asks that ominous question: "Dude, do you even remember what you did last night?" My heart sinks. My mind starts racing. I start thinking about all the crimes I possibly could have committed. It's the worst feeling. I got that call from a buddy once and it turned out that the night before, I grabbed a girl's tit right in the middle of the bar. And it was Claudio's girlfriend. And it was the first night I'd ever met her. And that's how I introduced myself.

ETIQUETTE

In a way, the entire act of going out and drinking is full of contradictions. I make a conscious effort to get drunk enough to the point where I can no longer make practical decisions, but not so drunk that I end up unconscious. In short, self-control is not easily learned, so here are some tips on how to know when you've had a few too many. You know you're wasted when . . .

➤ You stand in the elevator for ten minutes wondering why nothing's happening before realizing you never pressed any buttons.

➤ You can't figure out why you can't see straight even though you took ten tequila shots, didn't eat dinner, and donated blood earlier.

➤ You're in a crowded bar and you lose your motivation to avoid walking right into people.

➤ You come home from the bar, watch *Lost* on DVR, and the next day can't remember anything that happened in the episode.

➤ You get drunk Friday and miss work Monday.

> ➤ You meet a chick at the bar and put her number in your phone, but when you look at it later, it only has six digits.

> ➤ You get home from the bar and combine leftovers from two different nationalities. If you're dipping kung pao chicken into guacamole, you're wasted.

BOOZE AND CONSEQUENCES

You may remember Christina from *Ruminations on College Life* as my friend who cut her head out of a picture in which she held a drink in each hand, because that was the most sober picture of herself she could find for her med school application. Now that she's an anesthesiologist, several nights a month Chris has to be on "back-up call," meaning she doesn't have to be at the hospital, but she has to be ready to get there at a moment's notice if needed. Back-up call can be torturous, however, because essentially it's a day off, but you can't get wasted, which defeats the purpose. Christina reluctantly occupies herself with sober activities on these days because it was her lifelong dream to become a doctor. Personally, I just couldn't handle it. Still, there's something comforting about knowing that if I go out drinking but choke on an ice chip, there will be sober albeit bitter people like Christina available to nurse me back to health.

Doctors can be useful in other ways too. One of my weaknesses is that I am prone to particularly vicious hangovers. Since I hit my late twenties, when I go out hard on a Saturday night, I'm hungover until about Wednesday. Christina has promised me that the next time we party together, in the morning she'll give me a "banana bag," which is an IV in my arm full of fluids and multivitamins that they give alcoholics, and that doctors administer to themselves to cure hangovers. I don't know what's weirder—that I'm really looking forward to getting hungover, or that this is the first thing I've ever seen on *Grey's Anatomy* that is actually true.

BLOOD IS THICKER THAN ALCOHOL

In *Ruminations on College Life*, I wrote about how, when I was an undergrad, my mom mailed me an article from *Time* magazine about excessive drinking on campus. There was no money in the envelope, no letter, just the article. Many years later, I wrote in my column a story about drunkenly trying to close a tab at a bar before realizing I never put my card down in the first place. My mom responded with the following email, which I am quoting verbatim: "Aar, I enjoyed this one. One question—when you open a tab, it requires you to give your credit card over to the bartender? That is not very safe. People can make copies of your card and use your number to purchase items." I read the email and shook my head in disbelief. After a decade, I had finally allayed my mom's concerns about my drinking. But replaced them with fears of identify theft.

The final sign of voluntary alcoholism is denial. The morning after a bender, I feel like shit. I try to go through the motions of my day, but end up lying in my bed in the fetal position, reduced to eating one nibble of toast every fifteen minutes. Then, mercifully, about two hours later, I throw up everywhere. And when I'm finally done vomiting *Exorcist*-style with no regard for life, limb, or porcelain, I mutter to myself, "Must have been some bad toast."

These days, I find myself actually scheduling my hangovers. My dentist's office recently called me to set up an appointment a month away and I said, "Well, that morning doesn't quite work for me. The night before I have a wedding, so the next day is blocked off for a hangover that I just can't work around."

After my last major stand-up tour wrapped up, I suffered for weeks with a nasty cough. I finally dragged myself to my doctor in West Hollywood, who proceeded to prescribe me acupuncture. After trying to explain to her that normal people from the East Coast don't believe in that hippie shit, I relented and made an appointment. While he was sticking me with needles, the acupuncturist noted that my liver was slightly swollen and suggested that it might be caused by "emotional pollution." "Nah," I said, "it's probably the binge drinking."

I DRINK, THEREFORE I AM

I've always wanted to film a documentary where I go thirty days without drinking alcohol and see how much weight I lose, how much money I save, and how many girls I'm suddenly unable to speak to. It would be called *Sober Size Me*. When I described this idea to a friend of mine recently, she called me childish. I respectfully disagree. Alcohol's effectiveness as a social lubricant is well documented, and the vast majority of networking and courtship takes place in bars. Each weekend we dutifully traipse from the shittiest dives to the trendiest velvet ropes in search of a spot where everybody knows your name—but forgets it by morning. Maturity and drunkenness are not mutually exclusive in my opinion. In fact, the older one gets, the more important it becomes to get rip-roaring shitblasted on occasion. It's like chicken soup for the soul. Except, you know, the soup gets you really fucked up.

Our taste in alcohol reflects the phases of life. In high school, partying meant waiting until one of my friends went on vacation with his family, and then throwing a bash in his vacant backyard. Soon, we're stealing anything we can from our parents' liquor cabinet—God forbid we should go to the mall without a flask full of Rumple Minze. The indoctrination continues in college. Each spring, universities across the country hold various festivals that in reality consist solely of undergrads trying to get as fucked up as possible— as they tend to do whenever a tent, band, or carnival ride is involved. We develop a taste for cheap beer, boxed wine, vodka in a plastic bottle, and liquor with gold flakes or cinnamon chunks floating in it. After college, the drinking does not subside, but its effects must now be concealed. Business-casual-clad graduates trudge to work every morning knowing, if they must do it, which bathroom stall is the best one to boot in. We become somewhat more refined (I don't remember much of 2002 owing to a torrid love affair with dirty martinis), then more picky (these days, I pretty much only drink Goose on the rocks), until finally we're older, more mature, and imbibing upmarket, unidentifiable brown liquor served in snifters.

In a sense, though, DBD is more than just a personal admonition—it's a universal motto for all those who rightfully believe that your twenties and thirties should be a cherished time. A time spent finding yourself. Drunk. And in the beds of strangers. But drinking isn't always about excess and irresponsibility. Countless relationships have been forged over cocktails on a first date. Groundbreaking ideas have been spawned after a few beers. And I'm not just saying that because I'm wasted.

I recently woke up on a Saturday morning feeling very strange. I was unusually refreshed, but couldn't figure out why. Then I suddenly realized it—I wasn't hungover. Unfortunately, while abstaining the night before had made me feel physically better the next day, in my mind something felt amiss. The thing is, when someone asks me if I'd like a drink, I often hesitate for a brief moment before deciding. In that moment, the angel and the devil argue as I subconsciously extrapolate that one drink into the fifteen drinks that will inevitably follow. If vomiting and/or hooking up with a wideclops is an acceptable next-day scenario, I quench my thirst with a cold Amstel and let the bloodbath begin. After all, when you're trying to live the dream, the worst thing you can possibly hear is a buddy proclaim, "Dude, you missed a great night."

CHAPTER 6

A GIRLFRIEND INDEED

Every relationship that does not
raise us up pulls us down.
FRIEDRICH NIETZSCHE

My twenties were not an unbroken string of weeklong binges and one-night stands. Even I, champion of the freedom and independence that accompany bachelorhood, have succumbed to the Dark Side and been in serious relationships. I understand if it's difficult for you to picture me with a girlfriend. Sometimes I don't know how it happened myself. When I observe my friends' relationships, they seem to occur instantaneously—my buddy mentions a chick he banged and next thing I know they're moving in together. But when I have a girlfriend myself, time seems to stand still. In those weeks and months when a casual hook-up slowly evolves into a full-fledged burden, I begin to get a much clearer picture of what is expected of me as a boyfriend: sharing (don't like it), compromise (not good at it), and sacrifice (not worth it). I like to think that I do provide a valuable service, though. I'm sure my ex-girlfriends have, by now, realized that dating me is as hard as it's gonna get. I'm kind of like the heavy doughnut that base-ball players swing to prepare before stepping to the plate for real. I hope they'll thank me some day. Nonetheless, when I look back, my time in the relationship trenches has taught me to appreciate being single more than ever. The grass is only greener when you can fuck whoever you want.

A BRIEF HISTORY

My early relationships were a mixed bag. I dated my girl-friend in high school for only a few months before she broke up with me. I never did get a reason and haven't seen her since the day we graduated. Sometimes I imagine that I'll run into her somewhere random and she'll give me the "it wasn't you, it was me" explanation. But knowing what I know now, it was probably me.

Things went a bit better with my girlfriend in college. We dated for a little over a year before I broke up with her. Col-lege relationships are tough to gauge in hindsight because everything takes place in a vacuum and we were really drunk for most of it. I'm not even really sure why I broke up with her, though I'm willing to bet the potent combination of cock-iness and callowness that all frat boys possess had something to do with it. She's now married with her first child. So I guess I dodged a bullet on that one.

After graduation I was single in New York for a few years before I met my next girlfriend who, for the purposes of this book, we'll call Amanda. (For those of you scoring at home, in *Ruminations on Twentysomething Life* and in my column, Amanda is only identified as "Girlfriend.") As my first relationship after college and still the longest one I've ever had, I consider my time with Amanda to have been especially eye-opening. Alas, after a year and a half I moved to Los Angeles, she moved to Atlanta, and that was that. Again, if you're scoring at home, that brought my record in break-ups to one win, one loss, and one tie.

I found myself single again for a couple of years, this time in Los Angeles. One day I got a call from Amanda, who told me she was moving to LA. A few weeks later, I ran into her at a local bar. Incredibly, that night, only about five feet away from Amanda, I ended up meeting a girl we'll call Claire and subsequently started dating her. It was almost as if a symbolic torch had been passed from Amanda to Claire: "I put up with this neurotic asshole on the East Coast; I now bequeath that honor to you on the West Coast." Though she still lives in LA, I haven't seen Amanda since that night. I broke up with Claire nine months later, and that's when the itch *not* to get married began.

When all was said and done, I spent about seven years of my twenties single and three years in relationships. I had plenty of time to sow my wild oats and fuck indiscriminately, but also learned what it means to be a boyfriend and attempt to care not only about myself. And while I have fond memories of both Amanda and Claire, there were certain aspects of both our relationships that soured me on having another one for quite some time. They, on the other hand, got over me quite quickly.

FIRST KISS TO LAST CONDOM

I was introduced to Amanda through a mutual friend from my Wall Street days, and the first time we ever hung out was with a bunch of people at a dive bar on the Lower East Side. Our first kiss was a drunken dance floor make-out session that portended our reputation as quite the inebriated couple. As it turns out, Amanda not only doesn't remember our first kiss, she doesn't even remember being there that night. Very romantic.

I also hooked up with Claire the first night we ever met (seriously, who goes on dates anymore?). Our relationship evolved a bit slower than mine did with Amanda. For one, Claire is a lot younger than me; coincidentally, we both went to Penn, but she had only recently graduated when we met. In truth, the age difference didn't really matter, but it was odd being in a relationship when one of us was still so immature, constantly drunk, and spending too much time on Facebook— and the other had just graduated.

Of course, the progression from just meeting someone of the opposite sex to being in a serious relationship with them is a long, difficult, and confusing process. I generally classify two people as "hooking up" once there has been an exchange of three consecutive, successful late-night texts. Thus, the hooking-up stage essentially means you have a "preapproved booty call." What I find amusing about this stage is that the guy always naturally assumes there's no way the girl he's hooking up with is hooking up with anyone else, yet he wouldn't think twice about hooking up with someone else himself. Essentially, we hold women to higher standards than we do ourselves. Which seems about right.

Once you hang out with the person you're hooking up with under one of the following conditions—outdoors, during the day, or sober—you're now "seeing" them. Seeing someone is basically equivalent to what my parents would call "dating"—more serious than casual, less serious than exclusive. Though for practical purposes, all "seeing" really means is that you're no longer completely embarrassed to be spotted with the other person in public.

OBSERVATION

The downside of seeing someone is that oftentimes other people will assume your relationship is more serious than it actually is. The most awkward leading question a fledgling couple can ever get from a third party is, "So are you twooooooo . . . ?" Cue sideways glances and uncomfortable silence.

The next stage is being exclusive. Now the difference between seeing someone and being exclusive is purely sexual. One night you're going at it in bed and the girl whispers, "You should put a condom on now." And the guy replies, "Oh shit. I don't have any more." He then pauses, shrugs his shoulders, and asks innocently, "Can we just do it anyway?" The girl ponders her options for a moment before finally responding, "Well, are we exclusive?" To which the guy says urgently, "Fine, sure, whatever!"

THE G-WORD

It's always important to know where you stand in a relationship. Like let's say I was with a girl for six months or so,
and then all of a sudden we found ourselves stranded on a
deserted island. And these crazy, violent, savage natives at-
tacked us and captured us and tied us up and started threat-
ening, "We're gonna kill your girlfriend!" I'd be like, "Whoa,
please, listen, just calm down! First of all, she's not my
girlfriend."

After being exclusive, though, the next stage is in fact officially becoming boyfriend and girlfriend. A lot of people get
confused here. How can you be exclusive but *not* be boyfriend
and girlfriend? Well, the distinction is simple: when you're
exclusive, you're only sleeping with one person, but you don't
yet have the complete 24-hour obligation to deal with all her
bullshit. My friend Holly was driving with her dog once when
a bee got in the car, sending both Holly and the dog into a
hysterical panic. As she swerved in and out of traffic while
trying to simultaneously swat the bee and calm her dog, Holly
decided that her next course of action should be to call her
boyfriend. What the fuck is he supposed to do about it? Just
pull over, bitch!

Women are like biologists, always wanting to classify
every little thing. When I discuss these "stages" of relationships in my stand-up act, I've actually seen chicks taking
notes. They want a clear delineation of what's going on. Guys,
for the most part, act a lot more on instinct when it comes to
defining their relationships. The first time Claire left me a

voicemail and said, "It's me," I knew we had leapt to the next level. Later that week she went out while I stayed home, but when she couldn't find her friends at the bar, actually called *me* for help. Shit, that means it's serious.

GLOSSARY

RELATIONSHIP EXTRA-VALUE MEAL

When I'm in an exclusive relationship and decide it's time to move to the next stage, I usually formally ask the girl to be my girlfriend. I've always thought that was a nice touch, just to make it official. I asked Claire to be my girlfriend on Valentine's Day. Some of my friends thought this was cheesy, but what they didn't realize was that, from then on, every year, our anniversary would fall on that holiday—which would be convenient to remember and enable me to combine two gifts in one. I call it the "relationship extra-value meal."

PARENTAL CONSENT

Once a couple goes from just casually hooking up to seeing each other, that's usually where the guy's and the girl's views of the relationship start to diverge a bit. The girl starts telling her mom about all of our dates together; meanwhile my mom has no clue this chick even exists. My mom is pretty much on a need-to-know basis until the day before my wedding, when I'll be like, "Mom, get a dress!"

One time I called a girl I'd hooked up with and she happened to be at her parents' house visiting. I heard her mom walk in and the girl say, "Oh, hey Mom, I'm just talking to Aaron." *I'm just talking to Aaron?* She already told her mom about me? Besides the fact that I wasn't sure if this girl's name was Jennifer or Jessica and she was listed in my phone as Sergeant Sloppy Tits, how did she even tell her mom we met? Because I'm pretty confident she didn't say, "Well, Mom, I was at this bar downtown, totally wasted, and when they turned the lights on at 3 a.m., Aaron was the closest guy to me. Turns out he was just as drunk as I was so I ended up going down on him."

LIKE FATHER, LIKE SON

My mom is especially nervous about my dating prospects because I'm loud, grumpy, and keen on getting my way at all times—pretty much an exact replica of my dad. She once said to me, "I feel bad for any woman who goes out with you. I know what it's like—I'm married to you."

My mom, of course, has a checklist of all the requirements she believes the right girl for me should have. These days, however, I can tell she's really widening the net. If I tell her I met a girl who doesn't meet any of her criteria, and is in fact the polar opposite of everything she ever wanted in a daughter-in-law, Mom still looks at me, smiles, and says, "She sounds wonderful."

Everyone's parents also have that one friend of yours whom they want you to end up with, even though it's never going to happen. For my parents, it's my friend Marcia, who happens to be happily married. But my parents have not given up hope. "How's Marcia doing?" they'll ask. "Have you spoken to Marcia recently?" "You should probably fuck Marcia." Dad!

Whenever my sister Caryn or I bring home a significant other to meet the family for the first time, my parents like to fire a few shots across the bow to see if the newcomer can hang. My dad loves to cook and is a Food Network fanatic, so he'll analyze what a girlfriend orders at a restaurant and question her choices: "Sea bass, huh? What, you don't eat steak?" Little does she know that, as long as she responds with conviction, there are no wrong answers. Though if my dad has a few drinks in him, there are really no right answers, either.

My parents didn't meet Amanda under the most conventional circumstances. It was after a show at a comedy club in the West Village. Amanda was drunk. My dad was drunk. Even my mom was drunk (the rule said "two-drink minimum" and she always follows the rules). I had just spent the last seventy minutes onstage talking about sluts and blow jobs and then had to introduce everyone while standing outside on the sidewalk. The three of them were so hammered, tired, and cold that the pleasantries only lasted a few minutes before my parents left. In other words, my plan worked perfectly.

THE FIRST YEAR IS THE HARDEST

Some describe the first few months of a relationship as the "honeymoon period" because everything is fresh and new and easy. That's generally been the case with me, though things tend to take a turn for the worse pretty quickly. I can pretty much divide all of my relationships into three stages: the first few months are bliss, the second few months are a little rocky, and the last few months are spent trying not to get punched in the balls.

When I've been dating a girl for six months or less, I spend my time watching out for guys like, well, me. Because even the most sophisticated bachelors will still consider my girlfriend available. I know when *I'm* hitting on a girl at a bar and she tells me she has a boyfriend, if I can fight the urge to simply walk away, I'll ask how long they've been dating. If she says, "Five months," I'll be like, "Five months? Oh, phew. I thought you said you had a *boyfriend*. Sorry, that doesn't count."

GLOSSARY

FARTONOMY

The autonomy to fart whenever you want. Usually the first privilege a boyfriend gives up upon entering a relationship and the first right a husband takes back upon getting married.

One of the major issues I run into during the first few months of a relationship is acclimating myself to my girlfriend's menstrual cycle. The beauty of being single and never hooking up with the same chick more than a few times is that you're usually not around for twenty-eight days, and thus don't have to deal with unannounced hormone flux. The only time a girl's period even comes up is when she uses it as an excuse to thwart my tasteless advances. Once I have a girlfriend, though, every month for a few days I'm all of a sudden dealing with a completely illogical woman who is so convinced she's right, I begin to question myself. And that's what's so amazingly powerful about menstruation: it actually makes *me* feel crazy.

The other cycle of primary importance to a relationship is sex. When you first start dating someone, ever single night that you're together, you have sex. You're like the Cal Ripken Jr. of relationship banging. Then, one night, a few months in, the guy whispers, "Baby, I'm *really* tired tonight." And the girl says, "It's OK, baby. We don't have to have sex." And you both go to sleep and—boom!—your sex life is never the same after that. Your routine is soon reduced to one, maybe two positions (if she's drunk). The order is always the same: me on top, her on top, me on top so I can finish. The mere suggestion of trying to spice things up is met with such apathy: "Baby, you wanna maybe try, I don't know, doggie style?" [Long sigh.] "I guess." Finally, your dirty talk becomes so unoriginal: "Um, you smell good." "Thanks. Uh, so do you." "Did you DVR *Lost*?"

When my relationship with Amanda reached about eight months, we tried planning a vacation. But the only time we could both get away was four months later. This was a delicate situation. In essence, when I put down a deposit for the hotel, I was also asking for a 50 percent advance on our relationship. Given my past investments, that didn't seem like such a smart transaction.

When a relationship begins to pick up steam, it is soon tested by a series of holidays and milestones. The first is Valentine's Day (unless you used it to anchor your relationship extra-value meal, in which case you're off the hook for twelve months). To me, Valentine's Day is like that scene from *Indiana Jones and the Temple of Doom* where the villain rips out a guy's still-beating heart and shows it to the frenzied throng. For Valentine's Day is a day when men are forced to publicly demonstrate their feelings for the gratuitous pleasure of overzealous women. And given the opportunity to celebrate Valentine's Day or be eviscerated and thrown into a flaming trench, most men would surely choose the latter. I mean, at least evisceration doesn't require a reservation six weeks in advance.

Instead of spending two hundred bucks to go to some club that would most definitely suck, we decided to throw a party at Amanda's apartment for our first New Year's Eve together. It was very exciting. Not because I saved so much money and got to hang with Amanda and all of our friends, but because this was the first time in history I kissed someone at midnight whom I hadn't met only forty-five minutes earlier.

GLOSSARY

FBD

FBD, or First Birthday Dilemma, is the hurdle of having to figure out what message you want to send the first time your significant other celebrates a birthday. When Amanda and I dated, my birthday came first, which was tricky for her. She got me an iPod (this being back when iPods were still relatively new). My first thought was, "Whoa, I can't believe she got me an iPod; this is awesome!" My second thought was, "Oh shit, I need to spend twice as much on her as I was originally planning."

WORLDS COLLIDE

Women always want to show off their boyfriends: "Come on girls, gather 'round. This is my new boyfriend, Karo. Look at him!" It's like I'm a fucking circus animal. My girlfriend turns to her friends and whispers, "If I get him drunk, he'll dance!" Now, I only like meeting my girlfriend's friends for two reasons. The first being to find someone to fantasize about while I'm fucking my girlfriend. We all do it; it's standard operating procedure. (Though, guys, I advise you to rip out this page of the book so that your current or future girlfriend doesn't read it. The first thing she'll ask you is which one of her friends you think about. You do not want to have this conversation. Trust me.)

The second reason I like meeting my girlfriend's friends is to open up a new pool of chicks for my buddies to hit on. Every girl's got that one friend who's just a total fucking wreck. She's a chain-smoker with a throaty voice, her hair is always disheveled, she's a borderline alcoholic, but she's still pretty hot, dresses well, and has low standards. The first time we meet, she stumbles up to me, cigarette in hand, and shouts in a gravelly voice, "Hey Karo! So great to finally meet you! Got any cute friends?" And I'm just thinking to myself, "She'll do."

The "cross-pollination" phase of any relationship is tricky. This is when all my single friends start asking me if my girlfriend knows hot chicks, and all of my girlfriend's friends are asking her if I know cute boys. Soon, they all meet, a few from my side hook up with a few from her side, drama ensues, and everything gets a little awkward. Luckily, everyone on both sides is usually immature enough to simply avoid each other until it eventually blows over. I still contend, however, that a relationship is not officially serious until one of my friends bangs one of her friends. That's when you know you've got real chemistry.

WOMEN BE SHOPPIN'

I refuse to go shopping with a girlfriend. Actually, let me rephrase that. I refuse to go shopping with a girlfriend when *she* needs to buy stuff. Having to wait outside the dressing room while she tries on outfits is so inhumane it should be against the Geneva Conventions. Though I kind of like the depressed looks that single women give me when they leave the dressing room and see me waiting there. I can just tell how desperate they are to have a boyfriend they too can subject to this torture.

Once I went to one of those vintage T-shirt stores with Claire. She kept pulling shirts with slogans from '80s TV shows off the rack and proclaiming how "random" they were. Um, it's a fucking thrift store; everything is twenty years old and, by definition, random. Now if she found a brand-new Thomas Pink button-down dress shirt hanging on the rack, *that* would be random.

Being sent to the drugstore to buy my girlfriend toiletries is another harrowing experience. One time Amanda sent me to CVS to pick up a few things for her. As I warily made my way through the skin-care aisle, I could not believe how many ointments and gels they make just so girls will think they look better than their girl friends. While shopping, I actually saw something called de-ageifying lotion. I don't even think that's a word.

GO WITH THE FLOW

The one and only time I bought tampons for a girlfriend, I wrote down exactly what she needed and brought that piece of paper to the store. While vainly searching for the right pad things or whatever, I noticed a really cute chick also buying feminine products. I showed her the piece of paper and asked if she could help me. I've honestly never hit it off with a girl as quickly as I did then. She laughed at all of my jokes. Fucking irony.

Whenever Amanda would come back from the store, she'd have a new copy of *Us Weekly*. I would make fun of her about it incessantly. That is until I had to take a shit in her apartment and my need to read on the can outweighed my hatred for celebrity gossip. I grabbed a copy and went to work. Little did I know what I was in for. That magazine just sucks you in. Within ten minutes, I knew more inane minutiae about Shia LaBeouf and Angelina Jolie than I did about . . . well, than I did about Amanda.

I, on the other hand, buy my groceries online and have them delivered each week. Claire thought that was the strangest thing ever and always questioned why I didn't just go to the market. "Go to the *market*?" I'd ask. "What am I, the fucking big toe?"

Amanda was obsessed with selling things on Craigslist. While she was at work, she'd make me wait at her place for the guy who bought her stuff to come over and pick it up. She'd say, "I don't want to be alone with some random stranger." And I'd be like, "Well *I* don't want to be alone with some random stranger either! Why is my life worth any less than yours? Believe me, if that dude tries to kill me, I'm just gonna *give* him your CD rack! Fuck that."

FIGHTER NOT A LOVER

Everyone knows that couple who fight every second they're awake, thereby annoying everyone they come into contact with. The strange thing is that fighting couples are never self-aware—they don't realize that they're *that* couple. Here's how you know you're a fighting couple: if you regularly get into an argument with your significant other about one of you being either sensitive or defensive. Because that's a fight you inherently can't win and that will always lead to more fighting: "Why are you so defensive?" "I'm not defensive!" "See? Exactly." Or: "Stop being sensitive!" "I'm not being sensitive!" "Well, you *sound* pretty sensitive." And the circle of fighting continues.

OBSERVATION

Ever notice that girls will make you promise not to do something before they even tell you why? Your girlfriend will say, "If you see my ex-boyfriend at the party tonight, promise me you won't get pissed off." "Why?" you ask. She's like, "Just promise you won't get pissed off." "Fine, I promise. Why?" "He tried to kiss me last night." "Are you fucking kidding me? I'll kill him!" "You promised!" "Argggh!"

One of the most delicate situations in a relationship is when you're going out for the night without your significant other. Because even though you discussed it and it's totally not a big deal, when you're walking out and she says, "Have a good night," you always perceive the slightest tone in her voice, and then ask the dumbest question possible: "Are you mad at me?" That inevitably leads to a five-hour argument, a box of tissues worth of crying, and one entire night ruined.

That's what's so annoying about having a girlfriend: you're now responsible for another person's happiness. Fuck that. When I go to a party, I don't even want to be responsible for the camera.

The only moments of humor I found in all my fights with Amanda and Claire were when we were getting into it while out to dinner. There's nothing like awkwardly calling temporary timeout on a heated argument because the waiter has approached the table. I'm pretty sure that all waiters know that the phrase "We just need another minute to look at the menu" is couple code for "No one is getting laid tonight."

A BOYFRIEND IN NEED

I wouldn't classify myself as high maintenance per se, more like just a pain in the ass. I'm still not sure how my girlfriends were able to put up with me. For instance, I really don't like talking on the phone. Call to ask me a question? No problem. Five-minute call just to say hello? Understandable. A little chatting before bed? I'll deal. But there's no fucking reason to be having fifty-minute conversations in the middle of the day. I'm busy, woman! My Bluetooth should not be overheating from talking to you. Plus, girls will never proactively end a conversation. I have to be the one to initiate the "OK, baby, I gotta go." I'm convinced that if you don't make the move to wrap things up, your girlfriend will never, ever get off the phone and will just take you along with her all day, like some sort of audio-only reality show.

I even get annoyed just taking a walk with a girl. Because the thing is, women like the *concept* of wearing high heels but not walking *in* them. Much of a girl's decision-making is based around how much her feet hurt. If she's wearing heels and the place you're going to isn't within a fifty-foot radius, you can bet you're taking a cab—ironically to CVS to buy more Band-Aids for her fucking toes.

ETIQUETTE

Sorry, but even if I'm in a relationship I will continue to constantly adjust and scratch my crotch. All guys do it; it's genetic. It's a package deal that comes with our, well, package.

I also try to force my interests on my girlfriends, such as when I made Amanda watch hours of Yankees baseball against her will. I figured it would be worthwhile to teach her a little about my team and its players. While doing so, I discovered that Amanda learned about baseball at almost exactly the same rate as my four-year-old cousin. My conversations with the two of them were remarkably similar: "OK, who's up at bat now? No, not A-Rod, but close . . . Hi . . . Hid . . . Hidek . . . That's right—Hideki Matsui! Good job! And what's his nickname? Come on, I know you know this . . . Godzilla, right again! Good girl! Now let's get you some ice cream."

BAD COHABITATION

Since living with Brian after graduation, I resolved never to live with anyone ever again, at least until I get married. I just can't stand having another human in my fucking personal space. After Brian and Blake got their own place, I moved from our old apartment, which was just a few blocks from Amanda, to a studio that was across the street from her. I could literally see her bedroom from mine. People asked why Amanda and I didn't just move in together. Well, for me, the negatives outweighed the positives. The positives were that we'd both save money and she had DVR at the time but I didn't. The negatives were that I'd have to kill her.

Another drawback I've noticed about living with your significant other is that the bedroom always skews girly. Triplet #3 lives with his wife, and their apartment is modern and well decorated. But once you cross the threshold into their bedroom, things get frilly and purple real quick. And I have a feeling it wasn't Trip 3's idea to buy forty-six pillows for the bed, including a dozen of those cylindrical ones that serve no purpose at all. Some evil mastermind must have made a fortune off of those.

Even worse was what happened when my friend Marcia first moved in with her boyfriend (now husband). She said their schedules were so hectic that, in order to save time, they showered together. Every single morning. I told her I had an even better solution. It's called "move out."

In some respects, having a girlfriend but not living with her is the best of both worlds. On those nights when you're not together, you can leisurely browse Skinemax before bed instead of snuggling and watching *Will & Grace* reruns. But perhaps the most drastic change in my life resulting from having a girlfriend is that masturbation becomes a special time. It's usually such a common occurrence. But once I'm in a relationship, it becomes so rare that, if I find myself with seven minutes of alone time in my apartment, I have to savor it. I dim the lights, I burn some candles. All I need is some de-ageifying lotion and I'm good to go.

There was a brief period of time after Brian and I moved out and before I moved across the street from Amanda when I actually moved back home to the suburbs with my parents. I would, however, spend every weekend in the city with Amanda. One Wednesday, I had a meeting in Manhattan, so I told Amanda I'd take her out afterward as a special midweek treat. She got upset. Why? Because I was coming into the city partly for business and not solely because I wanted to see her. In other words, just spending time with her was not sufficient. There had to be pure male sacrifice involved. I now know never to use the word "convenient" when making plans with a woman. Instead I just substitute the phrase "you're beautiful." That seems to work.

HEY JEALOUSY

If I'm going to a bar with a bunch of my boys, even if I have a girlfriend, the first question I'll ask is, "Are there going to be any hot chicks there?" Why do I care if I'm not looking for ass? Well, some people like bars with microbrews and indie music. I like bars with hot chicks everywhere. It's just for atmosphere. The same sort of sentiment holds when I'm having a friendly conversation with a girl at a bar. Once she says she has a boyfriend—even if I have a girlfriend—I kinda just don't want to talk to her anymore. No hard feelings; you're just no longer as interesting as I thought you were.

One time I was at a bar with Amanda and some of my friends. Me, Amanda, and Triplet #1 (who was single at the time) were hanging out when Trip 1 spotted a couple of cute girls sitting by themselves. Trip 1 wanted to talk to them but we couldn't find any of our other friends and he needed a wingman. So I asked Amanda if I could try hitting on them, just to see if I was rusty or not. She laughed and stood back to observe as I completely crashed and burned. You know how embarrassing it is to get shot down by a chick in front of your girlfriend? Because you know she's wondering, "How the hell did I fall for that bullshit?"

For the most part, I'm not the jealous type. If I'm dating a girl and she wants to go out with an ex-boyfriend who's in town, I always give my blessing. I guess I just tend to feel secure in my relationships. The problem is, chicks want their boyfriends to feel a little jealous. But why would I? To me it's a pleasant treat to have some other dude buy my girlfriend dinner every once in a while.

However, if my girlfriend is going to hang out with her ex-boyfriend, I'd rather not know anything at all about him. Keep me in the dark. Having the details, for some reason, actually does make me start to feel jealous. I remember I was talking to Amanda once and she said, "Did I tell you I ran into my ex-boyfriend Jeremy in the street the other day?" And I was like, "Oh man, I didn't want to know his name. *Jeremy?* His cock must be huge!"

NOT GOING THE DISTANCE

In the scheme of relationships, long-distance is the worst thing ever. I don't care what anyone tells you. It never works, it doesn't make you "stronger," it's just a plain old-fashioned clusterfuck. I probably deal with it worse than most people. Amanda and I broke up only a few weeks after trying to do long-distance. Though she later moved to LA, we never got back together. Possibly because I think Santa Monica and West Hollywood are far enough away to still be considered long-distance (it's eleven miles).

I was once told that long-distance saves you a lot of money, because you're no longer taking your girlfriend out to dinner and paying for her all the time. Besides being an incredibly tenuous case in favor of long-distance, it's not even true. Flying to meet your significant other is expensive. Plus, each time you visit each other, every night out is a special occasion and thus costs a pretty penny. Long-distance actually costs *more* than a regular relationship. So don't spend all that money on plane tickets and shipping gifts when it's not even gonna last. Instead, invest in someone more geographically desirable. Or a Wii.

GLOSSARY

DOUBLE LONG-DISTANCE

Occurs when both parties move simultaneously, as when I moved from New York to Los Angeles to pursue comedy and Amanda moved from New York to Atlanta for advertising school. This was an especially difficult situation to deal with since we were both starting new lives in new cities, and frustrating because we were both frequently visiting New York even though the other person wasn't even there anymore. Also known as "long-distance with a twist."

Amanda and I tried everything possible to make things work after we both moved away. I even bought us webcams. It was great just to be able to see each other, but the webcam sex was a little disappointing. It was kind of like watching streaming porn that's constantly buffering and the audio is three seconds behind the video. Eventually, though, we got back into our old habits. Turns out arguing over a grainy, choppy Internet connection is just as effective as arguing in person.

The truth is, though, the cracks in my relationship with Amanda began to show way before we ever tried long-distance. For instance, she could never hear me on my cell phone. I don't know what it was; my reception was fine with everyone but her. We just got so frustrated every time we spoke that a fight would break out. But I refused to try to fix it because I really liked my phone. "Blame T-Mobile, not me!" I'd say.

Then of course there was the time Amanda asked me if I loved Derek Jeter more than her. I probably should not have responded, "Well, I've known him longer."

THE BREAK-UP

One thing I have never done is cheat on a girlfriend. I never cheat. Probably because I'm too lazy. You have to come up with an alibi, you gotta sneak around, it just seems so tiring. Plus, I'd probably do something really dumb like go to the other chick's house and then update my Facebook status to say where I am. And let's face it, cheating is really just a cowardly way to end a relationship when you're too much of a pussy to simply break up with the person. Some guys just want to get caught. Like my buddy who cheated on his girlfriend—while on vacation with her. Subtlety is not his strong suit.

After trying to cope with double long-distance, Amanda and I realized the end had come. Our break-up was sad, but very much amicable and mutual. (I think; with the webcam it was hard to tell if she was crying or choking on a pretzel.) With Claire, things didn't end as smoothly, mostly because it was a more unilateral decision. I wanted to break up with her as delicately as possible, so I decided the best way to do it would be over the phone. My thinking was that she would be less upset if she didn't have to see me in person. Big mistake. I think she was madder at me for doing it over the phone than for breaking up with her. So we met in person later that day and I did it again. This time it took. Lesson learned.

The first order of business after a break-up is telling your friends and family what happened. This is terribly painful. Not so much because it's the end of a beautiful relationship, but because it's so annoying to have to tell the same story repeatedly. I remember when my cousin told me she had just broken up with a guy she'd been dating for several years. I was the first person she told, and as she began to get upset, all I could think about was how many times she would have to tell the same story to different people. I could just imagine the coming weeks and how she would have to repeat herself over and over again— the same boring, drawn-out explanation of what happened for every person who asked. The horror.

Men and women of course react completely differently when you tell them you've just broken up. Girls are like, "Tell. Me. Everything." Guys are like, "Just gimme the gist. And make it quick; the game's on." Women empathize. They want to know if you're OK and how you're feeling at that very moment. They ask, "Is there anything I can do to help?" Men exult. They congratulate you and welcome you back to the workforce. First order of business: get you laid.

AMBITIOUS IDEAS

You know those annoying emails that people send asking you to update your contact information for their records? What would really be great is if you could add relationship status as a field. You could take care of everything with one email blast: "My fax number is the same, however I am now available to bang any of your cute co-workers."

The ability to efficiently disseminate word of your new-found availability already exists to some extent on Facebook. In fact, the first administrative task many newly single people do is remove the In a Relationship tag from their profile (or sign up for an account to begin with). Women will also go online to get post-break-up intelligence, including analyzing the status updates of their exes for deeper meaning ("Oh my God, his Facebook status says 'just chilling.' How could he just be chilling!?") and searching for patterns in their wall posts ("Who's this girl who posted on his wall like four times in one day? I've never seen her before; fucking slut!"). The great irony is that these days we're so connected it's easier to end an offline relationship than it is to end an online one. We can break up but we can't log off.

THE AFTERMATH

Break-ups are tough. Well, at least for the girl. When it comes to relationships, guys are like a light switch; they can immediately shut their feelings off. Girls are more like a dimmer; their feelings slowly fade out. Every guy has gotten a voicemail from a recent ex-girlfriend that goes something like: "Hey Trevor, it's me. Allison. You know, me. Can I still say 'me'? Oh, I don't know; it's awkward. Anyway, I was just calling because I was driving and I saw this vin-tage T-shirt store and it reminded me of you. And then, guess what happened. A bee got in the car! Remember that? Good times."

It's tough talking to my ex-girlfriends right after we break up, even if everything is cordial, because I have to be really careful to avoid saying shit that I would normally say to a regular friend. For instance, an ex will ask me what I did Saturday night and I'll be like, "Not much. Went out and got pretty drunk. I met this chick and totally nailed— uh, nailed her shelves to the wall. Yeah, you know how tricky IKEA can be . . ."

Tactfulness is a two-way street, though. It's respectful to make the other party aware of what's going on, if only to give them the courtesy of not being the last to know. A while after we broke up, Amanda got wasted, then texted me to ask if I looked at other girls when we dated, since her current boyfriend apparently had a wandering eye. Which would have been fine had her drunken text message not been the first time she ever even mentioned she had a new boyfriend.

Following a break-up, the first thing a guy has to realize is that, no matter what the circumstances, she *will* move on eventually. A few weeks after breaking up, if you ask a guy if he thinks his ex-girlfriend is hooking up with anyone else, he'll always say, "No way." Ironically, this is the exact same sentiment that grips a guy in the early stages of preapproved booty calls. We simply cannot fathom the possibility that a girl has other romantic interests besides us. A guy could be invited to his ex-girlfriend's wedding, watch her exchange vows with her fiancé, and turn to his buddy and say, "Dude, she's totally still into me."

It doesn't get stranger than hanging out with an ex, especially if you haven't seen her in a while. I had dinner with Claire recently at a restaurant in Beverly Hills whose outdoor tables bordered the sidewalk. There were fucking street vendors walking back and forth trying to get me to buy flowers for her. One guy actually said, "Come on, man! If you have a beautiful girlfriend, you gotta buy her flowers!" I gave him ten bucks just to leave us alone. When I got home, all of my buddies asked how dinner went. My female friends asked how Claire looked. My male friends asked if I banged her. Some things never change.

Strangely, my time spent in relationships and my time spent being single have made me realize that, in some ways, the two are not that different. They're both all about timing. If you meet a girl when you are about to leave and move across the country, you're much less likely to successfully date than if you meet that same girl when you've just arrived and are ready to settle in one spot. Just like if you meet a chick at a bar at 10 p.m. when you're sober, you're much less likely to get head than if you meet the same chick at 3 a.m. when you're both wasted.

While we were dating, I once asked Amanda about her long line of ex-boyfriends. She said to me, "Boyfriends are like internships. I learned a little bit about myself from each one and then moved on." I laughed at the time but now am desperate to find out what she could have possibly gleaned from our relationship. Personally, I now know that I'm nowhere near being prepared for commitment, and that if you're not ready to change cell phone carriers for someone, you definitely should not be her emergency contact. In hindsight, then, Amanda's analogy is quite perceptive. To me, girlfriends are also like internships—in that I've merrily half-assed my way through both.

CHAPTER 7

FOOLS OF ENGAGEMENT

> Marriage is the only adventure open
> to the cowardly.
> VOLTAIRE

My experience with weddings began in earnest in August 2006 when Brian and Christina—two of my oldest childhood companions—got married only five days apart. The floodgates had opened. It was then that I realized my friends would soon be divided into two opposing contingents: those eager to tie the knot, and those who merely think of weddings as really extravagant open bars with cover bands. I quickly became a grizzled veteran of wedding season, observing from the ever-shrinking singles table as my ilk—those who rock ill-fitting rented tuxes and try to bang bridesmaids—became increasingly ostracized. Now, each summer, as my engaged friends busy themselves with ballroom dancing lessons to prepare for their first dance as husband and wife, while I prepare toasts and speeches making fun of them, I can't help but wonder what possesses an otherwise rational man in his twenties to get down on one knee. Of course, with a bachelor party, a rehearsal dinner, a wedding, a couple of pregnancies, and sometimes a divorce thrown in for good measure, the engagement is merely the beginning of a multi-year series of events that's made me recognize that marriage is truly a wonderful thing—when it's not happening to you.

SPREADING THE WORD

I was at a party when I told my buddies that my cousin Rob had proposed to his girlfriend at the finish line of the New York City Marathon the previous week. The response was mixed. One friend said, "Proposed? I don't even like sleeping in the same bed as my girlfriend." Another remarked, "Girlfriend? I can't remember the last time I banged the same chick twice." And my personal favorite: "Marathon? I don't even have a gym membership!"

If there's one thing about getting engaged that seems really annoying to me, it's not picking out the ring or planning the surprise or even the subsequent lifelong commitment—it's telling everyone the news. I mean, obviously close family and best friends get a personal call. But what about everyone else? I've actually gotten most of my engagement news via text message. Which is fine, as long as you actually have the person in your phone book and don't have to text back: "congrats! who is this?"

As with kicking game, however, texting always has the potential for miscommunication. One of my first friends to get engaged was my frat buddy Joey. We were trading text messages while he was out boozing in Miami, and then I didn't hear from him for a few hours. When he finally messaged back, he wrote: "i'm engaged!" I responded: "lol! how drunk r u???" Turns out he wasn't kidding.

Spreading the word via text is a slippery slope. When Triplet #1 proposed, he sent even his closest friends a mass text that simply read: "yo soy engaged." Very classy. Then there's the case of one of my fans in Boston who opted to inform his buddies he was getting engaged as part of a trade request on their fantasy football message board. The guys approved of his marriage proposal but rejected the trade.

THE RUSH

In 2003, I emceed a speed-dating event at a bar in Manhattan. (I'm still not sure if this was sadder for me or the participants.) Much later, I found out that two people who went to the event because they were fans of my column met each other there and got married less than two years later. Besides feeling dirty for enabling this union (though the pay was pretty good), I couldn't help but wonder, what's the rush? How do you go from just meeting someone to walking down the aisle in twenty-two months? I've never even *dated* someone that long.

Of course, not everyone is in such a rush. Most people have that one friend who's been dating a chick for like eight years but refuses to even discuss the possibility of marriage.

I love provoking these guys because they always overreact. I'll say, "So, hear about Joey? I guess you're next, huh?" And he responds, "Whoa, whoa, whoa, not even close! I'm not even thinking of considering even maybe getting engaged! Possibly a few years from now. I want to take it slow. Very slow. Really, really slow. Like unnecessarily, painfully protracted, drawn-out slow—that's the kind of slow I'm looking for."

But as much as I like prodding my hesitant friend about when he's going to propose, I love hanging out with his girlfriend even more, especially if she's the only one among the couples we're with who's not engaged or married. I always feel a sense of camaraderie with her. She'll ask, "What's new, Karo?" And I'm like, "Not much. You?" And, surrounded by others' wedding bling, she sighs, "Nothing." And then we both get drunk, secure in the knowledge that neither of us is getting hitched any time soon.

In the end, though, I believe marriage is the great equalizer. You have to understand, ladies, our entire lives since puberty have been predicated on waiting for you. Guys are always ready to hook up, but we don't get any unless one of you decides "the time is right." But when a guy is thinking about proposing, that's the first, last, and only time he holds all the cards. My, my, my, how the tables have turned. If I had a girlfriend I was thinking about proposing to, I would relish it for as long as possible. I'd buy a ring and then wear it on my cock. And then get a tattoo that read: "Ain't payback a bitch?"

> ### *GLOSSARY*
>
> **OBSESSED-WITH-GETTING-MARRIED CHICK**
> We all know an OWGM chick; she's got the ring picked out and the venue booked. If you moved in with your boyfriend less than six months after you started dating, sorry, but it wasn't "just more convenient," it was because you're trying to fast-track the relationship. I pity OWGM chicks (and the guys they emasculate) for missing out on the joys of single life. And I have some advice. To me, finding your keys, hooking up, and getting engaged are similar: they all happen when you're not thinking about it and least expect it.

At the beginning of 2007, Brian and I made a wager. We created a spreadsheet in which we guessed when each of our four friends then in serious relationships would get engaged during the year. Whoever was more accurate would be taken out to dinner by the other. If wagering on the romantic relationships of our friends seems absurd, perhaps even offensive, then I'm willing to bet you're in a relationship yourself, or you're my mom. The fact is, those of us not in the race because we're not getting married soon (me) or because we've already been eliminated (Brian) really have no moral qualms about it. And if you're gonna be in such a rush to propose, the least you could do is time the most important decision of your life around the indiscriminate date I've chosen for you.

THE INVITATION

I always know that wedding season is right around the corner when people begin asking for my mailing address. That can only mean that invitations are on the way. For the past five years, besides wedding invitations, the only use anyone has had for my physical address has been the occasional pre-game at my apartment. Of course, sending my address out then didn't prevent the twenty drunken phone calls from friends that night asking, "Yo Karo, where the fuck do you live again?"

My frat buddy Jay sent out wedding invitations that actually had a typo. He and his fianceé had to send corrections with the right date. I wasn't able to attend but I saved the invite just in case it's worth something one day—like a baseball error card. Still, that didn't compare to when I got my college girlfriend's wedding invitation in the mail a few years ago. She was getting married to another guy from my fraternity. I knew she was engaged, of course, but seeing the actual invitation kind of freaked me out. I mean, that could've been me. And there's no way I would have picked such nice calligraphy.

GLOSSARY

NEAR-MARRIAGE EXPERIENCE

This is the sensation I felt when I found out my college girlfriend was marrying the guy she dated immediately after me. It was like my single life flashed before my eyes. All those random blow jobs that never would have happened. It was terrifying.

When Brian was getting married, he suggested to Blake that they put an email address on their wedding invitations in order to save money by not using reply cards. The idea was met by quiet sobbing and quickly quashed. I don't know why guys even try to participate in the wedding planning process. Of all the "Save the Date" notices on my refrigerator, my favorites are the ones that feature a picture of the happy couple, because I like to imagine what the conversation was like that led them to include that photo on the card. I usually envision the girl looking lovingly into her fiancé's eyes and saying, "Honey, we're gonna take a picture in which I look beautiful and you look awkward, send it to everyone we know, and you have absolutely no say in the matter."

The four most important components of the wedding planning process are: when to hold the event, where, how many people to invite, and who. Let's get one thing out of the way right off the bat: unless you're only inviting like fifty people, if you have your wedding out of the country or on New Year's Eve, you're an asshole. Plain and simple. Who to invite is a touchier subject. I love when people complain to me that a friend hasn't invited them with a "plus one." I believe the correct terminology is "guest." You're not on the list at a fucking nightclub.

If you were born in the summer, like me, you've probably already prepared yourself for a lifetime of disappointment. No cupcakes in elementary school. No parties in your honor in college. And now, even the best-laid birthday plans are constantly disrupted by a never-ending string of engagement parties and weddings. Honestly, all I want for my birthday this year is to have been born in March.

THE REGISTRY

The wedding registry combines one of my favorite things—online shopping—with one of my least favorite things—buying overpriced gifts for people making poor decisions. I almost always buy alcohol-related items (or "barware," as those fancy fucks at Williams-Sonoma call it). The way I figure it, that's the only way I'll be able to partake in my friends' usage of the gift. Of course, I've never actually drunk anything from a flute or carafe. But I figure as long as there's an opening at one end, the beer will know where to go.

ETYMOLOGY

A little-known fact is that the term "adding insult to injury" was actually coined to describe the act of buying something off the registry for one of your friends, only to be added to that store's mailing list and receive unwanted catalogs for the rest of your life.

To some, the wedding registry is merely an opportunity to say, "I like you guys this-many-napkin-rings much." I, for one, still get insulted when I buy something from an online registry, but the address where the gift is headed is blocked out for "privacy concerns." Listen, if I'm giving you something called "stemware," I want to know exactly what apartment it will never be used in.

Oftentimes I'll give the couple a gift but get a thank you card written only by the wife, whom I'm barely friends with. And it's always written in really neat, girly handwriting that barely conceals the fact that she fucking hates me. It will usually imply something along the lines of: "Dear Karo, Thank you for being a part of our wedding and not vomiting until after the ceremony. We really appreciate the shotglasses as well as three of the four napkin rings we registered for. Also, thank you for organizing the bachelor party for Ted. By the way, he admitted you paid for him to get a hand job from a stripper, and I've forgiven him. Just wanted to let you know that when we have kids, you're not allowed anywhere near them."

FOOLS OF ENGAGEMENT

Once I received a voicemail asking me to call the local courthouse and confirm my appointment for a marriage license. Given the fact that when I listened to said voicemail, I was in bed next to a girl whose last name I did not know, I was pretty sure it was a wrong number. Being the Good Samaritan that I am, though, I called up and explained the mistake. Consequently, somewhere out there is a couple whom I assisted, albeit indirectly, in getting married without complication. There are days when I regret my decision to help out, for one simple reason: engaged people during the run-up to their wedding are some of the most insufferable humans on earth.

Guys, if you're engaged and sitting around with a bunch of single dudes swapping hook-up stories, don't chime in like, "I had the best sex last week." I don't care if you banged her in the ass on one of those swings they advertise in the back of *Maxim*— no one wants to hear about you fucking your fiancée.

Engaged women, on the other hand, are always running around chirping, "*Oh my God*, everyone is *so* excited for the wedding!" Sorry, but that's just not true. Not everyone is excited for your wedding. I mean, your alcoholic uncle is excited for the open bar. But the chicks from your sorority who don't even really like you aren't excited. The people who have to spend five hundred dollars for a plane ticket to fly in from out of town—only to stay in the hotel where you've arranged for "special rates" so outrageous I can't imagine what the regular rates are—certainly aren't excited.

OBSERVATION

What is with the engaged couple always asking if I've booked the hotel they reserved for their "destination" (read: inconvenient/ expensive) wedding? No, I haven't booked the fucking hotel. I'm pretty sure those "special rates" aren't going away, as you claim. Plus, there's another reason I haven't booked a room yet. I'm planning on banging one of the bridesmaids in *her* room. See? Problem solved.

My main problem with traveling to weddings is that I treat it like a vacation. So my first night in town—be it at the rehearsal dinner or not—I get so blindingly drunk that I'm inevitably hungover for the ceremony itself. In fact, to this day I am wrongly blamed for getting so smashed at Triplet #3's wedding that I vomited in the parking lot during the reception. Fact: I hadn't even been drinking that much and was merely still ill from the night before, thank you very much.

It amuses me to no end that, when planning a wedding, the bride and groom pay so much attention to details that no one else even notices. Christina's wedding was on Block Island, which is an island between Rhode Island and Long Island, just off the coast of Bumblefuck. A few weeks beforehand, she called to ask me what ferry I'd be taking to get there. "Ferry?" I asked. "What ferry?" "The ferry to the island!" she exclaimed. "You know, it was on page four of the Save the Date booklet we painstakingly crafted for your benefit?" "Ohhhh," I said. "That thing. Yeah, I was using it as a coaster."

A few months before her wedding, my friend Marcia flew out to LA to hang out with me for a long weekend. To be clear, Marcia and I have never and—now that she's married—will never hook up. (Though she was my prom date, I must admit I couldn't seal the deal.) I have to confess, though, I did feel kind of strange about spending an entire drunken weekend with her. Like being engaged was some sort of contagious disease that I could catch. I had to remind myself that marriage isn't cooties.

ALWAYS A GROOMSMAN, NEVER THE GROOM

When Brian asked me to be his Best Man, I was both honored to serve and thrilled to have ammunition to use against him for the next year. When we started to argue over something like who had the better SAT II scores or who could run the forty-yard dash faster in eighth grade, I'd always interrupt and say, "Wait, wait . . . what kind of man am I? What kind of man? That's right, the *Best* Man. You said it yourself: the Best!" I started to wonder if one could get fired from the wedding party.

ADVICE

I'm sick of hearing bridesmaids endlessly bitch and moan about their dresses. Just think of it like Halloween—you're gonna dress up in something ridiculous, everyone will take pictures, and even if you look halfway decent, the only chance you'll wear that outfit again is at a party where no one saw you in it the first time.

My primary duty as Best Man was to organize the bachelor party. And organize I did, sending thirteen warriors to Las Vegas for a weekend they would never remember. The real pain in the ass was not so much the planning, but rather laying out money for everyone and then trying to get them to pay me back. It's not that my boys are cheap. It's that they're lazy and they're dicks. I had to call one guy every day for six weeks, and received a check from another buddy who for some reason found it necessary to write in the memo section the words "I hate you."

Triplet #1 recently got married . . . to another triplet. I know the odds are astronomical, but of all the chicks in New York City, he managed to find one from a set of female triplets. All six of the siblings are fraternal, so there was no risk of confusion. But Best Men and Maids of Honor were tagging in and out of that ceremony like some sort of black-tie WrestleMania.

SPEECH!

As a comedian, giving speeches is my favorite part of any rehearsal dinner or wedding. I prepare for them like I'm preparing for an actual gig, though it took me a while to realize that brevity is appreciated. Case in point: my never-ending, seventeen-minute Best Man "toast" at Brian's wedding. While it was relatively well received, the entire speech had to be included on the couple's 45-minute wedding video, since they hadn't contracted for such complex editing. Needless to say, no one wants me to take up 38 percent of their most treasured memories.

I guess I felt I could do no worse than Brian had done himself, when he served as the Best Man at one of his fraternity brother's weddings the year prior. Standing next to the groom and his, ahem, well-endowed wife, Brian closed his speech by accidentally congratulating his friend for choosing "the *breast* bride possible." Brian called me frantically from the bathroom of the reception hall right after the toast to tell me what happened. I calmed him down, but quite frankly I was thrilled to have been given a Get-Out-of-One-Inappropriate-Gaffe-Free Card for my own upcoming speech.

Little did I know that Brian's wedding would not be when I needed dispensation most. When Christina—whom I've known even longer than Brian—got married a few days after him, she held a clambake in lieu of a traditional rehearsal dinner. Oysters and lobsters as far as the eye could see. Unfortunately, I'm allergic to shellfish. After a dozen glasses of champagne on an empty stomach, Chris surprised me by asking me to make a toast. I grabbed the mic, started riffing on my dear friend, and about halfway through accidentally dropped an F-bomb on the crowd. Apparently, wedding speeches are not supposed to make babies cry and guests walk out.

But despite my personal string of snafus, I still believe that bridesmaids should never be allowed to make speeches. Honestly, they're never good. I'll even go so far as to say that, in my entire life, no girl has ever told me a story of any kind that was interesting or funny at all. Seriously, guys, if you and your girlfriend both witness an event, *you* tell me what happened.

And when bridesmaids give speeches, they always read directly from a folded-up printout of exactly what they're gonna say, like a fucking sixth-grade book report. What are you doing? Outline and memorize! I think the only way that girls should be allowed to gives speeches at weddings is if they tell the true story of how the bride and groom actually met. Typically, the story goes that Rachel was at a bar, she accidentally spilled a drink on Shawn, he got her number, their first date was in the park, and the rest is history. Bullshit. Here's what most likely actually happened: Rachel and Shawn met at a bar. She spilled a drink on him because she was wasted out of her mind. Shawn took her home but Rachel wouldn't fuck him—which is pretty much the only reason why Shawn texted her the next weekend at 2 a.m. Rachel finally put out . . . and the rest is history.

WHY WE'RE GATHERED HERE

I like the little program you get when you arrive for the wedding ceremony. I immediately search for the list of bridesmaids. For single guys, this is our first look at the menu for the evening. Sometimes, it lists the bride's relationship with each bridesmaid. And while the backstory is appreciated, all I'd really like to know is if she has a boyfriend and what my odds are of sealing the deal in the next, say, five hours. I was at a wedding once where two of my friends—who didn't know each other beforehand—ended up hooking up. Later, the girl asked me if it was weird that the guy tried to sleep with her. Dumbfounded, I replied, "It'd be weird if he *didn't* try to sleep with you."

The fact is, every guest at a wedding who is invited without a "plus one" is in search of an elusive and mythical bounty: wedding ass. As the thinking goes, combining lonely single people with an open bar at an event celebrating love should equal rash decision-making and no pants for everyone. But of course the theory that it's easy to get laid at weddings only holds true if there are actually available girls there. As I get older, each wedding I attend seems to have a smaller population of eligible bachelorettes. And you know the pickings are slim when even the singles table has fucking couples at it!

But that doesn't mean the marriage of a man and woman who love each other doesn't ever lead to premarital sex between a man and woman who barely know each other. I've done my share of damage, including two wedding weekends where I hooked up with two girls apiece. The first night is much easier, since guests are getting into town from all over the country and are eager to meet new people and party without inhibition. The actual wedding is a bit harder for me, usually because I have to spend at least until the cocktail hour avoiding the chick from the night before.

My primary target will always be the bridesmaids. Since the groom knows them, I'm able to gather better pre-wedding intelligence and, if I'm a groomsmen, jockey to get paired with the hottest single one when walking down the aisle. Plus, if one accepts that loneliness contributes to easiness, then surely the closer a woman is to the bride, the more desperate she becomes. Unfortunately, due to our large, still intact crew from high school, at Brian's ceremony the groomsmen outnumbered the bridesmaids by about three to one. So not only were there not enough chicks to go around, but as Best Man I had to walk down the aisle by myself like a lost drum major in a marching band.

THE BIG DAY

I was rushing to get ready for my high school buddy Seth's wedding when I realized the dry cleaner had given me back someone else's tux pants and they were five sizes too big for me. Since I was at my parents' house on Long Island, I didn't have any backups and had to cobble together a makeshift outfit from half a tux and half an outdated, unflattering suit from college. Only later did I discover the dry cleaner had accidentally switched my tux pants with my dad's, and mine were hanging in his closet in the next room. Which would have been funny had I not just spent the whole night looking like some kind of black-tie hobo.

Everyone says the big day is all about the bride. It's her time to shine. And thank God, because if weddings were focused on the groom they'd be twice as painful. Grooms always look so fucking awkward during all stages of a wedding—from the time they walk down the aisle right until the last dance. They're stiff, they're nervous, they look like they're about to faint. Sometimes when I'm sitting in the back of the ceremony with the rest of the degenerates who rolled in late, I just want to walk up to the groom, sit his sweating, anxious ass down, and take his place. Not because I'm desperate to get married of course; I just love being the center of attention.

After the ceremony and approximately six minutes into the cocktail hour of any wedding, I always have the same panicked thought: "There aren't enough bartenders." Seriously, if you can hire someone whose sole function is to make sure the bride's train doesn't touch the ground when she walks down the aisle, you can have someone serve me a fucking Goose on the rocks without making me wait more than a millisecond.

GLOSSARY

FREDDING

A wedding where many of the guests are frat brothers of the groom. Freddings often involve a lot more drinking and the occasional tuxedo-clad human pyramid. Brides, if your fiancé has worn an article of clothing with his fraternity's letters on it in the past thirty days, you're most likely having a fredding. Prepare for possible streaking.

Christina got legally married at city hall six months before her actual wedding, in order to exploit some loophole that allowed her and her husband—both doctors—to get placed in jobs in the same city. I thought the wedding weekend would be a little anticlimactic, but I was pleasantly surprised to get just as belligerently wasted as usual. The first night was the drunken clambake toast disaster, and the morning after the actual wedding I woke up outside in a hammock. The final tally? Bridesmaids taken down: two; tuxes ruined by hammock: one; memories I'll cherish forever of one of my oldest childhood friends getting married: zero.

During the reception, the bride and groom are like celebrities to me. They're the stars of the show, but they're mostly surrounded by their best friends, like a little VIP section. If you're not a VIP, you actually have to observe and plan out when there's an opening for you to go up and talk to them—as if you were looking for an autograph. Then you chat for like two minutes just to make sure they're aware that you did in fact attend, but you know they won't even remember it. Basically, the only difference between the groom and Justin Timberlake is that JT didn't spend the summer taking lame-ass ballroom dancing lessons.

WORDS OF WISDOM

"He who misses bachelor party gets twice as drunk at wedding."
—Ancient proverb I just made up

My move to Los Angeles coincided directly with the first wave of my friends getting married. Thus, since leaving New York I've played one of the most underappreciated roles at every wedding I've attended: the out-of-town guest. The simple truth is that flying in for a wedding is a huge pain in the ass. It's annoying, expensive, and forces you to make sacrifices (for example, having to choose the wedding over the bachelor party). But I soldier on anyway. Why? Because I enjoy celebrating with my friends. I want to be in attendance on the most important day of their lives. And I like making toasts (sometimes unsolicited and often laced with expletives). All I really ask of the happy couple is that they recognize the contribution that single dudes make to their wedding. Seat us next to the hottest available chick. Thank us for spending three hours on Kayak.com looking for a decent flight. Use our crystal serving thingamabob. But most of all, hire another fucking bartender.

POST-NUP

Hanging out with married people my own age is really strange. You know, because they're married and I'm still human. Guys who are about to get married are very fond of telling their boys that "nothing is gonna change; we're still gonna hang out." Trust me, everything changes. I remember talking to one of my buddies a few weeks after his honeymoon and saying, "Dude, all the boys are getting together. We're going on a mancation. We're going to fucking Mardi Gras. Are you in?" And my buddy was like, "I'm definitely in. Let me just ask my wife." I said, "You know what? Offer rescinded. Rescinded! There will be no permission-asking on this mancation. You ruined it."

Some guys become completely helpless once they get married, not so much because they ask permission from their wives, but because they rely on them to script their every move. I was hanging out with a female friend of mine, and her husband kept texting her, asking her what she was doing and complaining about being bored. His wife actually had to suggest that he make plans with friends and even offered to call them herself. So basically she was setting up a playdate. Seriously, dude? What did you do when you were single? Just do that, except don't have sex with anyone but your wife!

GLOSSARY

RCFs

Engaged and married people often hang out with RCFs—random couple friends. These are the groups of couples you've never seen before that all of a sudden occupy all of your buddy's time. Where the fuck did these people come from? When a man gets down on one knee does some high-pitched whistle sound that only boring couples can hear?

Many of the issues I have with married people stem from the fact that they only hang out with other couples. It's two by two by two by two—like a fucking Noah's Ark of boring dudes wearing loafers and chicks who own fondue pots. When couples congregate they start to get weird, crazy ideas that no single (read: sane) person would go along with. No, I don't want to go to your friend's wife's wine-tasting dinner party! I don't even know what merlot is!

Since serving in Brian's wedding party, my responsibilities as his Best Man have continued. Last year, he and Blake had to go to separate weddings on the same day. I happened to be going to the one that Blake was going to, so I essentially served as her "date" for the evening—sitting next to her and getting her champagne and generally looking out for her. She promptly got hammered, spilled a drink into her purse, and had to throw rocks at Brian's window when she locked herself out at the end of the night. Mission accomplished.

HUSBAND AND WIFE

The turnout for my ten-year high school reunion was surprisingly high. A few people got inappropriately shitfaced, but the highlight for me was running into my first girlfriend from middle school and meeting her fiancé. After all, when we dated for about a week circa 1991, who would have thought that, so many years later, one of us would be embarking on an amazing phase of life filled with thrills and new adventures—and the other would be getting married.

About a year and a half prior to my ten-year high school reunion, I attended my five-year college reunion. During the festivities, I wandered into a tent for those who graduated in the '80s, and noticed an unusual number of super hot chicks—which was surprising, because that's not exactly what Penn is known for. Then I realized that none of the name tags that the really hot women were wearing listed a graduation year. And that's when it hit me: these were actually the alumni's wives. Apparently, the Latin on my diploma reads, "Bachelor of Science in Economics with a minor in Marrying Well."

OBSERVATION

Dear Future Wife: The most important job you will ever have is to kill spiders for me.

If I could make but one desperate plea to married people, it would be this: Please *do not* get a joint email address with your wife. Honestly, what the fuck is wrong with you? Grow a pair and keep your own email address. It's not like sharing a car; it's free! There's no reason I should ever get an email and be confused about whether it's coming from my buddy or his wife: "Hey Karo, let's get fucked up tonight, you asshole! Warm regards, Kristin and Jonathan."

As I've already mentioned, I believe married people should not be allowed in bars. On top of the issue of forcing guys to look for rings on the fingers of girls they're kicking game to, married people are simply taking up valuable real estate. Engaged people aren't exempt either; what are you doing here anyway? Go home and pick out place cards or some shit. I don't even think married people should be allowed on Facebook, let alone in bars. If I ever see in my news feed that Jane Smith went from In a Relationship to Married, the next line better be: "Jane Smith has deleted her profile."

PREGNANT PAUSE

Just as I began to make peace with the fact that all my friends were leaving me behind by getting married, they took things to a whole new level and started popping out babies. I'm convinced that everyone's doing it just to placate their parents. My mom has never put any explicit pressure on me to get married and have her grandkids, but I can tell by her tone of voice that she'd appreciate it if I'd at least *try*. Whenever I mention the fact that I'm nowhere close to being ready, she just gives me the *look*—that look that says, "I raised you and put up with all your bullshit and you can't do this one lousy fucking thing for me?" Nobody likes that mom look. It just makes me feel bad about everything I've ever done in my entire life. But not quite guilty enough to actually do anything about it.

An executive I've worked with in LA recently had her first kid. Every time we see each other now, she has this glow about her that comes with being a new mother. Single guys, of course, have the opposite feeling. Any morning we wake up and *don't* have any children is a cause for celebration. I had a pregnancy scare once. A girl I was dating came over to my place and said, "I'm late." Confused, I looked at my watch and said, "Actually, you're early." Two hours later I was trying to decipher the cryptic results of a pee-soaked stick. It was negative. I breathed a sigh of relief. After all, the pregnancy test alone cost $21.99.

FALSE ALARM

My second pregnancy scare occurred when someone told me my college girlfriend just had a kid. I was like, "Oh shit, I slept with her nine . . . wait, nine *years* ago. Not months. OK, phew, that was close."

Gadi, my Israeli friend, just married a chick with an eight-year-old son. His wife is gourmet and Gadi and the kid get along great. Still, I don't think I could ever date a girl with a kid. I mean, if a relationship is gonna have an immature whiner who vomits without warning, it's gonna be me. Let's face it: I won't even date a girl who lives more than a quarter mile away from me. I won't date a Red Sox fan, a smoker, someone who doesn't watch *Lost*, or someone who doesn't drink. Hell, I won't even date a girl with a roommate, let alone one who sleeps in a fucking crib.

NINE LONG MONTHS

The weird thing is, I've started to feel sympathy pains when my friends are pregnant. Though when I say "sympathy," I mean I feel bad for myself for having to endure such nonsense. Listening to my pregnant friends update me on the status of their unborn children is just torture. How long will it be until someone just says fuck it and creates a Facebook page for their fetus? Sonogram for a profile picture. Favorite movie: *Look Who's Talking*. Interests: Mitosis. Birthday: Hopefully soon.

Even if you're single, being pregnant takes you out of the dating pool. You're not even eligible for consideration. I once called my gym to schedule a massage and the receptionist offered me a choice of three female masseuses. I half-jokingly asked her which one was the cutest, and she replied, "Definitely Amber." When I showed up a week later, I saw that Amber was pregnant. Very pregnant. Like eleven months pregnant. Either the receptionist was fucking with me, or she didn't realize that pregnant by definition means "not cute."

ETHICAL DILEMMA

Shermdog was on a crowded, rush-hour subway in New York when a pregnant woman waddled onto the train. As soon as he got off, Shermdog called and asked me if I thought it was wrong of him not to give up his seat for her. I said that I wouldn't necessarily classify that as "wrong" but that it would have been the polite thing to do. Then he added that, at the time of the incident, he had been wearing his scrubs and hospital ID. I responded that, well, in that case it may have been wrong. Then I asked, "What were you thinking?" To which Shermdog replied, "That she was hot and I kinda wanted to fuck her." Yeah, definitely wrong.

How come babies are never born in the afternoon? Every time I hear that someone had a kid, it's always at like four in the morning. I mean, I was born at 8:10 a.m. and I haven't gotten up that early since. Seth is the first of my high school friends to have a kid. His son, Logan, was born at close to midnight, which is at least a little more reasonable. It's really weird to think about how old Logan will be by the time I actually have kids myself. I really look at each of my friend's newborns as a potential babysitter.

OH BABY

The only thing worse than getting updates on my friends' unborn children is getting updates on their *born* children. My old boss on Wall Street used to tell me that his daughter would always get into this jar of candy they kept in the kitchen, so he finally put it on top of the fridge where she couldn't get to it. However, when he and his wife weren't watching, the daughter peeled off the bath mat from the tub, brought it into the kitchen, and pulled all the drawers out of one of the cabinets, creating makeshift steps to climb onto the counter. Then she used the bath mat as traction to climb onto a small shelf, and from there she jumped on top of the fridge and got to the candy jar. The whole time I was thinking, "That's not a three-year-old, that's a velociraptor."

AMBITIOUS IDEAS

I propose a pact: celebrities are not allowed to give their babies stupid names if the National Weather Service is not allowed to give hurricanes even dumber ones.

Because I've been writing my *Ruminations* column since my freshman year of college, my fans and I have literally grown up together. I share momentous events in my life— graduating from college, moving to Los Angeles—with my readers, and they do the same in their emails to me. Earlier this year, a longtime fan wrote me to say that she'd recently taken to reading my column while breast-feeding. Ugh. I thought I'd at least be turned on that somewhere out there a chick is enjoying my work with her tits exposed. Instead I couldn't drink milk for a week.

Babies love me. Babies always smile and laugh when they see me. But I don't think it's because I'm good with kids. I suspect they just think I'm funny-looking. Whenever I hang out with my young cousins who live near my parents in New York, it always makes me think about how great it would be to be a dad . . . if I only had to be with my brood in twenty-minute intervals and never when they pooped themselves or cried.

HE TAKES AFTER ME

When he was four, my sister asked our cousin Daniel if he had learned anything in school. Daniel replied, "Yes, but I can't say those words out loud."

As a comedian, I obviously travel a lot. I'm on a plane like every week. The one thing I fucking hate more than anything is when families ask me to switch seats on a flight to accommodate them. "What's that you say? You want me to switch seats with you because you're separated from your kid? Well, let me see if I can make myself clear: Go fuck yourself. Listen buddy, I booked this flight online, chose exactly the seat I wanted, and printed a boarding pass at home. Now you want me to sacrifice my own comfort just because you forgot to pull out? Not a chance. I don't give a shit if you and your wife and your newborn baby are sitting nowhere near each other. You should have thought of that ahead of time."

END OF AN ERROR

Of the four couples that Brian and I wagered on, only two got married; one couple is still not engaged, and the other broke up. Despite the adrenaline rush that must have both influenced and resulted from my cousin Rob proposing at the marathon, he and his fiancée subsequently broke off their engagement. In fact, I know about a half dozen people who have gotten divorced, separated, or un-engaged in the past year alone. Most are understandably upset. But the way I think about it, I can't even fathom making a commitment of that magnitude in the first place. So if you're my age and have already broken such a commitment, well, that pretty much makes you the coolest person I know.

My friend called me recently and asked if I knew any lawyers for her sister. I began racking my brain for all the guys I know who both went to law school and don't have a girlfriend. Turned out she didn't want to set her sister up with a lawyer, she wanted a referral for her sister, who was getting divorced. I said I could do that, too, but still secretly only referred her to my lawyer friends who are single.

One of my buddies who is on his second marriage was recently complaining to me about how fucking crazy his ex-wife is. But as he was going off, I couldn't help but wonder how he didn't figure this out ahead of time. I'm sorry, but if you date, live with, propose to, and marry a chick, yet still don't realize she's totally psychotic, you have no one to blame but yourself. And your idiot friends who knew all along but didn't tell you.

Maybe it's just denial on my part, but I still refer to my friends' wives as their "girlfriends" and continue to call my married female friends by their maiden names. While I don't wish it upon anyone, I figure, at some point, at least one of them will get divorced. And since I won't have to update her last name in my address book twice, I'm the big winner.

LAST MAN STANDING

If you want to make an argument for the beauty of marriage, take my parents, married thirty-five years and still going strong. When I moved to a new apartment after my first year in LA, they flew out to help and I was able to observe them closely as we spent four straight days running errands while I futilely attempted to get them to pay for stuff. What I noticed was that, after all these years, my parents are still looking out for each other. My dad made a point to make sure that the air conditioning was strong enough to allow my over-heated mom to sleep comfortably. And my mom would suggest we take a break to eat because she knows just when my dad is getting hungry. After a while, though, I realized these were not entirely selfless acts of adoration, but rather long-ingrained defense mechanisms. My dad wants my mom to be comfortable so that he can sleep without her tossing and turning. And my mom wants my dad to eat so that he won't get cranky and start aggravating her. So in essence, I believe the key to a happy marriage is identifying, isolating, and mitigating what your spouse does to annoy you.

Though I frequently mock the concept of marriage, it is still a wonderful institution that works out about 50 percent of the time. And I do hope that one day—many years from now—I will get married myself. I guess, as they say, we mock things we don't understand. And while I understand theoretically why the people I know are getting married, it's hard to fully comprehend that commitment when you're personally not there yet. That's why wedding season is sometimes bittersweet for me. For instance, Marcia's wedding was a little over ten years after we went to prom together. Since then, our lives couldn't have become more different. But, in a way, not much had changed in a decade. Once again, I found myself at the end of a long night—alone and in a tux—with nothing to do but jerk off.

My college buddy Harlan is someone I've always looked up to in terms of being a sloppy, unrepentant party animal. So when even he got married, I really started to feel like the odd man out. I also realized that getting married has at least one huge advantage that being single can never match: unlimited license to get as stupid as you want while always having someone there who's required to stick up for you. If Harlan gets plastered at a wedding, his wife can always step in and say, "He's with me." And people look the other way, knowing

Harlan has at least attained some minimum level of maturity. If I cause a scene, I'm looked down upon: "It's just some single guy who knows the groom. Don't worry; he'll be on a plane back to California in the morning."

The truth is, most of my past serious relationships began with a one-night stand. In fact, many of my married friends actually met their husbands or wives in what started as a casual hook-up and then unexpectedly blossomed into something more. Therefore, it's reasonable to assume that's how I'll meet my wife as well. So I figure the next time I try to take a girl home from the bar and she objects, asking, "What kind of girl do you think I am?" I can respond, "I guess not marriage material."

EPILOGUE

As I was putting the finishing touches on this book, I decided to sit down and reread my first book, *Ruminations on College Life*. (And, yes, by "sit down" I mean I was in the bathroom.) At first, I was a little apprehensive about looking back at my thoughts on bachelorhood, some of which were written when I was as young as eighteen. But I was soon comforted when I realized that my thought process has remained consistent all these years. "The thing about college," I wrote back then, "is that college kids don't really date so much as we randomly hook up." Turns out college me was a prescient little fucker.

Eight years after graduation, I'm still practicing what I preach—I'm just a whole lot better at it. To be fair, though, I have many more resources at my disposal now than I had at Penn. I didn't even have a cell phone until junior year and was still using dial-up when I was a senior. Hell, when I was in college, Facebook was an *actual book* that we used to stalk chicks. Then again, the generation before me didn't even have email. One can only assume they all graduated virgins.

When I was a freshman, I couldn't even imagine what it would be like to be thirty. But age is strangely a much more constricting factor within the bubble of a university. I remember I had a crush on this junior girl, but even entertaining the thought of kicking game to a chick two years older than me was laughable. Perhaps that's where the hubris of modern bachelorhood originates—from the vengeful angst we build up as hapless freshman guys. Today, a thirty-two-year-old woman wouldn't even faze me. She *wishes* I was interested in her.

I recognize, of course, that not everyone will agree with the sentiments I've put forth in this book: that being single is more exciting and fulfilling than being in a relationship, and that getting married in your twenties is akin to signing fun's death sentence. I suppose if you meet your soul mate right after college, continue to work hard, play harder, and maintain some semblance of the independent life you had before, all while enjoying the intimacy and camaraderie of a significant other, then you've beaten the system. I just haven't seen a lot of empirical evidence supporting this scenario. It's like an urban myth perpetuated by jewelers, dressmakers, TheKnot.com, and Williams-Sonoma.

In fact, I posit that the longer you're single before getting married, the better off you'll be, because only single people truly know what makes them happy. Unless you've spent years drinking your inhibitions away, putting yourself out there, experiencing the thrill of one-night stands, and coping with the agony of rejection, how can you really know yourself? Playing the field is merely doing due diligence while having a blast to boot. More importantly, what fun is married life if you don't have any hijinx to reminisce about? Waking up next to your wife every morning must be twice as reassuring after you've spent ten years waking up next to chicks you have to introduce yourself to.

When I graduated from college, my dad imparted several bits of advice to me, which I wrote down and have referred to ever since. One of his simplest tenets is the one I've taken most to heart: "Keep your options open." It sounds obvious, but I've found that many people don't follow it. I've adapted it to work on so many levels too. Career: follow the path that opens up the most doors down the road. Bars: pick one that's close to a few others in case the first one sucks. Chicks: don't get roped into hitting on one girl all night, much less think about getting tied down to one forever. The list goes on and on. Throughout my twenties, I tried to follow my dad's advice, and it served me well. If you fight for choice and don't commit until necessary, the right option should present itself. The other piece of advice I got from my dad? "Don't tell Mom I gave you this advice."

Much like I couldn't fathom being thirty when I was a freshman in college, turning forty seems a lifetime away from me now. But I'm also more excited for my thirties than I ever thought I'd be. I spent my twenties doing virtually anything I wanted. If there was a beer, I drank it. If there was a chick, I banged her (well, tried). I'm not certain what the next ten years will bring, but I do know that what constitutes living the dream is ever-changing. Right now, booze, chicks, and good times with the boys are what make me happy, and so I pursue those things with unmatched vigor. Years from now, it might be something different. But I'll always look back at being a bachelor in my twenties with no regrets. Sure, I didn't contribute much to my 401(k) or ever get invited to a wedding with a guest, but I can tell you this: I had more fun than anyone who did.

—KARO
AUGUST 2009
LOS ANGELES

ACKNOWLEDGMENTS

In the acknowledgments of all the books I've read, the author usually proclaims the work to be a "collective" effort, and the result of many uncredited "co-authors" without whom it would not have been possible. Fuck that. This book was a solitary effort and I spent months by myself slaving away at it. *I* made it possible. I do, however, have a sublime support system, and they deserve their due. I would like to thank the following people:

My sister Caryn, who has been editing my *Ruminations* column for the better part of a decade, and who also edited the proposal I used to pitch this book to publishers. Caryn, you are one of a kind. I love you and have always valued your opinion more than anyone's, which is why it's all the more painful when you tell me something sucks.

My parents, who continue to defy all logic by supporting my career choices, sitting through my obscenity-filled stand-up shows, and generally being pretty fucking cool. Mom and

Dad, I love you and thank you for endowing me with the confidence to do what I do. And just for the record, I've now written *three* more books than Caryn.

Kate Hamill, who, unlike my sister, actually got paid to edit this book, but nonetheless treated it like her own. If you were offended by anything you read, you would not believe the suggestions from Kate that I *didn't* include. Kate, you have a filthy mind but a sharp eye. Thank you for acquiring my work and helping me mold it into greatness.

Darren Trattner, my attorney and the longest-standing member of my Hollywood team. You would not believe the incredible amount of legal minutiae that's required for everything I do. It's his job to sort through the fine print and throw some elbows. Darren, it's been a long, strange trip. Thank you for investing your time in my future.

Peter McGuigan, my agent. Although this is my third book, it's the first time I've had a book agent. It's surprisingly a lot easier this way. Peter, thank you for taking me on and singing my praises to publishers around New York. The first time we met, you told me there was "a chick, Kate, at HarperCollins who is gonna buy your book." Right you were.

Michael Pelmont, my manager extraordinaire. Had he not introduced me to Peter, who introduced me to Kate, this book might merely be a pipe dream. But that's what he does best: send me to myriad meetings, 99 percent of which are a complete waste of time. Michael, thank you for believing in me enough to tirelessly seek that elusive 1 percent.

My friends on both coasts, who know they are running the risk of being written about every time we hang out. Some of you have become minor celebrities in your own right from frequent mentions in my column. Don't lie; I know you love it. All of you have been like a second family. Thank you for always being there to bring me down a peg.

Last but not least, my incredible fans across the country and around the globe, who have been supporting me for twelve years and counting. I cherish every email, wall post, and tweet I receive from you guys. Thank you for making all my hard work worth it. My career has been spent making you laugh; and there's not a luckier guy in the world than me.